W9-CQY-702

Top 25 Ways An IUL Can Secure Your Financial Future
(And Build a Tax-Free Family Bank!)

Mark J. Quann

with Josh Shapiro

THE REMii GROUP • LOS ANGELES

Publication design by Book Lab at booklab.co

For more information, orders, corporate discount plans, media and speaking engagements:

Orders: www.amazon.com
Facebook: www.facebook.com/remiigroup
Email: mark@remiigroup.com
Website: www.remiigroup.com

Also by Mark J. Quann

Rich Man, Poor Bank
Top 10 Ways to Avoid Taxes

Contents

A Money-Back Guarantee vii

Before You Read This Book 1

Is This Book For You? 3

Part One: Introduction to IUL

Why Now? 9

The Purpose of This Book 17

Why IUL? 19

    How Does It Not Lose Money? 19

    Whole Life Insurance (WL) 20

    Term 21

    Universal Life (UL) 23

    Variable Universal Life (VUL) 24

    Indexed Universal Life (IUL) 24

    The Fear Penalty 29

Part Two: 21 Ways to BUILD IT!

Lifetime Financial Planning 37

    1. Financial Indepedence vs. "Retirement" 37

    2. Use a Term/IUL Combination 39

    3. Inexpensive Long-Term Care (LTC) Insurance 43

        Will the Myths of Long Term Care Leave You Unprotected? .. 46

4. Cash Value Rises With the Stock Market, Never Falls!..47

5. Fear/Emotion Management.................................47

6. Forced Savings...49

7. Annual Lock-Ins or Every Two-to-Five Years (It's Up to You!) 50

8. No Cap Strategies...50

9. No Taxes During Growth 51

10. No Maximum Annual Contributions...................51

11. No Age Restrictions, or Requirements...............51

12. No Income Restrictions 52

13. "Rollover Minutes" 53

Beat the Big Banks 55

14. Build a Tax-Free Family Bank! 55

College & Education...61

15. College Funding 61

16. Pay Off College Loans 65

Business Planning..67

17. Key Person Insurance..67

18. Employee Retention..67

19. Buy/Sell Agreements 68

20. Employers Can "Discriminate" 69

21. Tax-Free Business Bank 69

Part Three: 4 Ways to PROTECT IT!

Protecting Your Retirement Accounts 73

22. Supplemental Tax-Free Retirement Income..........73

23. Tax-Free Social Security..........................77

24. Never Invest Conservatively Again! 81

25. Maximize Retirement by Minimizing Losses........83

Part Four: Your Legacy!

Legacy Planning (Bonus Way #26!) 91

26. Pass a Large Death Benefit to Your Family, Tax-Free and Probate-Free 91

    Don't Forget The Ring!................................ 93

The Top 10 Questions to Ask............................95

1. What is the purpose of this IUL for me?...............95

2. Is the insurance agent "captive?" 96

3. Is the insurance company publicly traded?...........96

4. What are the riders and their costs? 97

5. Is the Long-Term Care "indemnity"? 97

6. How high are the caps? Any uncapped strategies? .98

7. Does this IUL have alternate loan options?..........99

8. Cost vs Benefit. Can I supercharge it?.................. 101

9. Surrender Schedule (Is there a Prenup?) 101

10. What are my options for premium financing?..... 102

    Your Vows.. 103

Part Five: Conclusion

In Summary 107

Bonus Report....................................... 109

A Money-Back Guarantee

"I didn't mean to write another book. Really!"

Any author will tell you that it is both mentally and emotionally taxing to write a book. The writing. The rewrites. Then more edits and more rewrites. Then formatting. Then more edits, and more rewrites after the formatting. This tedious process seems like it will never end.

But I found myself answering the same questions about IUL ("Indexed Universal Life Insurance," in case you aren't familiar with the term) over and over again. My team was also getting the same questions, especially with the stock market falling. Normally I would refer them to a book that would answer the questions they were being asked. But despite the other books about IUL, written by CPA's and other authors, I had not been able to find a book that fully covered the many uses of IUL for both personal and business finance.

I sat down at home one day and started typing the top questions I had been asked. I had planned to write a "short report" to be read by our advisors and our existing and future clients. Four weeks later I was still typing and doing rewrites, and we began sending the report out to a number of clients asking for their opinion and feedback. We kept hearing the same response:

"I really learned a lot about investing and the markets reading it, is it okay to forward the draft to some of my friends? I think they would love it!" I decided to release the report first to our partners, advisors and many clients... and then release it as a book.

If you purchased this as a book or an eBook and don't think it is helpful and educational—and more importantly, you don't believe it will help you to secure your financial future—please send me an email and I'll refund you your money.

If you believe this book can help you secure your financial future, please take a moment and give it a (5 Star) review on Amazon.

Thanks!

Mark

Before You Read This Book

I would first recommend reading (or re-reading) *Top 10 Ways to Avoid Taxes*. It tells the story of how I was first introduced to IULs back in 2006.

Top 10 Ways to Avoid Taxes highlights the importance of using Other People's Money (OPM) in all your investing. If used properly, OPM can enhance your returns and supercharge all your strategies for building wealth. It covers the various ways to reduce taxes when investing in mutual funds, ETFs, stocks, bonds, and real estate. And, the best ways to pass wealth to heirs 100% tax-free.

Finally, it also introduced the concept of safely using OPM+OPM again, specifically when buying real estate, so that none of *your* money is in the investment. In this case, your real estate can be purchased with 100% Other People's Money!

This book will expand on even more ways you can use OPM in your investing, to generate even greater returns, all while reducing, managing, and sometimes eliminating risk.

I introduced the basics of IUL in *Top 10 Ways to Avoid Taxes* in a chapter I called "The Rich Man's Roth." If you would like a free copy of that chapter, send an email with the subject line "Chapter 6" to: **10ways@remiigroup.com**

If you have any questions after you read this book, send us an email and we will get them **answered.**

Is This Book For You?

I'm going to make some assumptions about why you're reading this.

My **first** assumption is that you have heard of IUL, and you are interested in it, but you also have some questions.

My **second** assumption is that you likely Googled "IUL" and you got mixed reviews.

My **third** assumption is that you may have come across the "talking heads" and "financial gurus" on TV:

"Life insurance is a bad investment."
"You should buy term and invest the difference."
"Max out your 401(k)—to save on taxes."

I've found this advice is better than no advice at all. But I've also found that the above advice will never build real WEALTH.

The #1 rule in my investing is simple:

If I can't use Other People's Money (OPM), it is not a good investment. PERIOD. No exceptions.

If you want to build real wealth, I suggest you adopt the same rule in all your investing. We will cover a lot more about this throughout this book, with everything you could possibly want to know about IUL. *My goal is that you will be far more knowledgeable than the vast majority of insurance agents and financial advisors on this topic.*

Here is one of the most common questions I get regarding IUL: *"How does an IUL perform when compared to the performance of the stock market?"*

We will provide you many examples of the power of IUL, specifically the incredible power of not losing money! But what I want to demonstrate is quite different.

What I want to show you is how IUL can fit into any investment portfolio and actually improve returns on your other investments, including your stocks, bonds, retirement accounts, and even your real estate or business.

Just like any insurance or investment product, IUL may not be a fit for everyone, but I believe if you understand the dozens of uses of IUL, it may benefit you in ways you never thought possible.

Let's see if IUL can help you build a more secure financial future.

The big questions we will attempt to answer are:

What is an IUL?
How does it not lose money?
How does it help me before I die?

But first, let's look at *why* this subject is so important.

In 2018, I wrote the following in *The Top 10 Ways to Avoid Taxes:*

As of today, in 2018, here is a summary of where we stand as a country:

- Almost a decade ago, the federal reserve printed trillions of dollars to try and save the economy.

- Just as I wrote about in *Rich Man Poor Bank,* that money is now "chasing the same amount of goods and services, causing prices to rise,"— inflation.

- Real estate and stock prices have been soaring, and I expect they will continue to do so for an unforeseen amount of time. But, as the saying goes, "Whatever goes up must come down."

Perhaps, like me, you are thinking, "When is the next crash coming, and how big will it be?" The answer is, no one really knows.

But with money skills, you should construct a plan to make money when stocks and real estate go up, and have a plan to make more money after they crash—buying more stocks and real estate when prices are low.

Have you heard the expression "buy low, sell high..."?

Lastly, while building wealth, it helps to understand that the economy only does two things:

It **expands** – causing prices to rise.

Or it **contracts** – causing prices to fall.

The best investors have a plan for both.

When picking your advisors, they should know how to make money in either case and be familiar with all ten of the tax avoidance strategies.

The bad news is another crash is coming. We just don't know when, or what will cause it.

But if you are one of the few that has lots of cash on hand, and money in IULs, a crash can be a great time to build wealth, especially when investing using OPM.

Remember, it is not "if" but "when" the market will crash next.

PART ONE:
INTRODUCTION TO IUL

Why Now?

If you recall, I started writing my last book in the intensive care unit of USC Keck hospital after having heart and valve repair. I had some downtime. For full disclosure, I'm writing this during the coronavirus pandemic. I have some downtime again, this time while in quarantine.

The stock market is breaking records for both declines and gains in the same week!

Down 10% one day, then up 10% the next!

Most investors are aware of the S&P 500, the index that measures the overall performance of the US stock market. But they are not aware of the index that measures FEAR. There is such an index, called the "VIX." (VIX is the ticker symbol for the Chicago Board Options Exchange's CBOE Volatility Index. It measures the stock market's expectation of volatility based on S&P 500 index options.) It is also sometimes called the "Fear Index."

When this index is very high, investors are generally driven by two emotions: Fear, and Greed.

When fear and greed are at their highest, investors typically sell low, then buy high, and sometimes even sell low again, with devastating results on their investment portfolios.

To give you perspective, I researched the history of the "fear index" at the height of the crash in the Great Recession, where it reached 79. The fear index recently hit 85, the highest ever recorded!

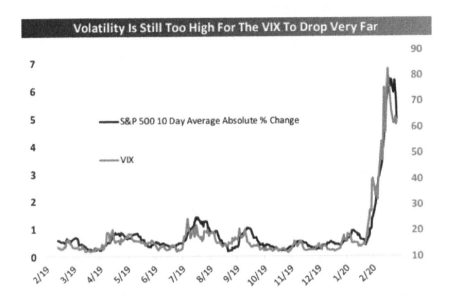

And it is possible the worst is yet to come, with over 3.3 million people filing for unemployment. It is estimated that 40+ million people will lose their jobs.

This causes fear to rise even higher.

Many investors looking for guidance turn for advice to the "talking heads" and the "experts" on television and the news.

On March 25th, two news reports were published within a couple of hours of each other:

CNBC's Market "Insider Report" had the Chief Investment Officer of Blackrock Investments commenting on the markets. The headline read:

> *"Bond volatility has peaked,*
> *and stocks may have hit bottom."*

The report went on to say:

"I don't think we will go back down under 2300."

The S&P 500 closed at 2475 that day.

The same day, Barrons.com published an article from a chief economist at a globally renowned independent research firm. The headline read:

"Why the stock market hasn't hit bottom
and could fall another 35%."

Who will be right?

My prediction: One may be right. One may be wrong. Or both will be wrong. It doesn't matter. *Both are just guessing.*

And when one (or both) are wrong, they will come back again as "experts" and, if asked about their prediction, they will say, "Well, I wasn't correct because of … [insert excuse here]."

Just two days later, on the 27th of March, a Barron's headline read:

"The Dow Just Had Its Best Week Since 1938.
It's Time to Go Shopping for Beaten-Up Stocks."

But wait! Two days ago your headline said it "…could fall another 35%." Yet people call their financial advisors and ask for advice. Like their financial advisor has a crystal ball.

Their financial advisor will give them the best advice they can give them based on historical data, market research, the history of the market, and studies of past investor behavior during market downturns.

"Don't sell now, stocks are likely on sale. Keep buying even when it is going down. In the long run it will likely go back up, and you will own more shares. This is called dollar-cost averaging. Don't forget it."

The stock market has overcome past bear markets and unsettling news
Growth of a hypothetical $100 investment in the S&P 500 Index (with dividends reinvested)

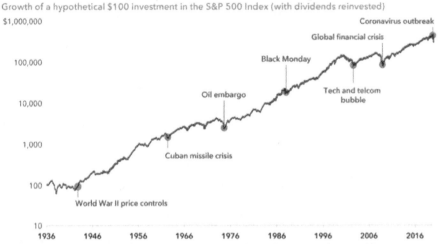

Sources: RIMES, Standard & Poor's. As of 3/23/20. Chart shown on a logarithmic scale. The Standard & Poor's 500 Composite Total Return Index is a market capitalization-weighted index based on the results of approximately 500 widely held common stocks, and assumes the reinvestment of all dividends.

Their advisor is correct, based on the historical data, market research and history of the market, and knowing that investors generally make bad financial decisions when emotions are high. FEAR is a powerful emotion!

But what many investors can't forget is the pain they experienced in past market declines:

The Peak – 2000

The S&P 500 closed in August of 2000 at about 1517.

It then crashed and continued its decline until September of 2002. It bottomed at around 800. *A decline of over 45%.*

I wasn't investing then, but I can't imagine watching my retirement account crashing in value...for almost 24 months!

The Peak - 2007

The market finally rebounded, eventually reaching a new highest ever, about 1545 in October of 2007 (up only about 2% from August of 2000).

The market started another steep decline and bottomed out February of 2009 at about 735.

Investors would be watching their accounts crash again...this time for another 15 months! *A decline of about 52%.* And yes, the market then began a bull run, and finally hit an all-time high.

To close out 2019, The S&P 500 climbed just above 3200!

CNBC ran a headline prediction:

"S&P 500 could see a breakout run to 4000 in 2020."

Wow! A strong economy, and optimism so high! What could possibly go wrong? You know what happened next.

To summarize, if you were an investor 20 years ago, you had to ride all the ups (exciting) and downs (fear) of the market.

And, to get the full *average returns of the market*, you needed to:

- Never stop funding it, at any time
- Never sell during a market decline.

If you sold during a downturn or stopped funding your account after a market decline, you would not get the "average returns of the market."

So, what did the market do during this period? It was at about 1500 in March of 2000. And **briefly** rose just above 3000 at the end of 2019. It took **two decades** to double in value. That is an average compounded rate of return of about **3.6%**!

Yes, this is excluding dividends, but it is also excluding the crash that we're now experiencing.

S&P 500

Certainly, we don't know what will come of the coronavirus pandemic, or where and when the market will hit another bottom. Only time will tell. I won't be making any predictions.

What we do know is that the government will once again "print TRILLIONS of dollars to try and save the economy," just like they did in the Great Recession.

And when the stock market recovers, fueled again by trillions of dollars, we could see another market recovery, followed by another boom, and yes, eventually another crash.

In my lifetime I truly hope we don't see another Great Depression, where the market lost 90% of its value. But with the United States in 24+ trillion dollars in debt, Medicare drastically underfunded, and the Social Security Trust Fund running out of reserves in 2034? I think it is a possibility.

During the Great Depression, it took 26 years for the markets to recover to their previous high. Can you wait 26 years for your portfolio to recover?

As I sit at home writing this, while also having a number of conversations with clients and the advisors that I train, I feel fortunate that I have stable income, multiple streams of income, reserves for short and long-term, and investments that did not lose money.

While most other advisors are taking calls from scared clients, I just received another "thank you" text from a client. Since 2013 he has been funding a significant amount of money each year into an IUL.

The text read:

> *"Mark, I'm sooooo glad I have my life insurance*
> *that doesn't dip below 0%. Everyone is going to make*
> *a ton on money when this swings back up!*
> *Hope you are well man!!!"*

When I called him back, my client wasn't scared at all. In fact, he was excited!

We discussed all the great opportunities to invest, now that the markets have crashed, and stocks are "on sale."

The Purpose of This Book

The purpose of this book is **NOT** to tell you that what you are doing is incorrect and you should not invest in the markets.

The stock market is a valuable tool for building wealth, and it will continue to do so long after the coronavirus pandemic has passed.

This book has 4 objectives:

1. **To educate you about the innovation in IULs and the many benefits. Including:**

   • Grow money in the market, risk-free and tax-free. Protect it from taxes, inflation and market declines.

   • Access your money tax-free at any age.

   • Pass wealth to heirs tax-free.

   • And many, many more in this book!

2. **To educate you about strategies to provide inexpensive permanent life insurance, and long-term care for asset protection, and pay for it with tax-free profit.**

3. **Show you how to build your own "Tax-Free Family Bank," and be able to borrow for the purposes of:**

   • Paying off real estate,

   • Funding college expenses,

   • Buying real estate (more effective after a market decline),

   • Paying off debt with tax-free earnings,

   • Investing in the markets (more effective after a market decline),

   • Providing supplemental tax-free retirement income,

- Protecting your 401(k) from running out of money in retirement, and...

- Do all the above with OPM—the most powerful strategy used by the TOP 1% to build great WEALTH!

4. **Educate the many financial advisors that are searching for strategies to help their clients build and maintain financial security.**

Why IUL?

How Does It Not Lose Money?

Throughout this book, I am intentionally going to be repetitive where I believe the message or lesson is very important to understand. Some of this material may also overlap parts of *Top 10 Ways to Avoid Taxes.*

In Chapter 6 of that book, "The 'Rich Man's Roth'," I wrote about how I discovered IUL.

I'm assuming you requested Chapter 6, you read it, and have a general understanding of IUL.

Indexed Universal Life, or "**IUL**" is regulated under Internal Revenue Code (IRC) 7702 and 7702a. This tax code, last revised in 1988 regulates how much of your after-tax money can be funded into a permanent life insurance policy.

There is really no cap to the annual amount you can fund into an IUL, as the larger the policy, the more you can invest!

IRC 7702a regulates all types of cash value life insurance policies, including:

- Whole Life Insurance (WL)
- Universal Life (UL)
- Variable Universal Life (VUL)
- Index Universal Life (IUL)

We will also cover how term insurance fits into your planning.

Let's jump into the exciting history of insurance! And see what brought IUL to the forefront.

Whole Life Insurance (WL)

Whole Life dates back to the 1940's.

These policies "cannot lose money," similarly to an IUL, which is great news when markets decline.

But what about when the markets recover, or go on a bull run with returns of:

23.45%	in	2009
12.78%	in	2010
13.41%	in	2012
29.60%	in	2013
11.39%	in	2014
9.54%	in	2016
19.42%	in	2017
28.88%	in	2019

WL will **not** participate in any of the upside potential of the market. It will only pay an annual dividend based on current interest rates.

And, the dividends paid to policyholders in WL insurance has been dropping for 30+ years. Many WL policies which paid dividends of 10%+ in the early 1990s, are now only paying dividends of 5% or 6%.

WL insurance has historically been sold by "captive" insurance agents, meaning those agents can only sell the company insurance policy that you see on their business card. We will talk more about this later in the book, but doesn't that seem like a conflict of interest?

Yes, it is true WL works well to **preserve wealth and protect you from taxes**.

But an IUL can **preserve wealth, substantially grow wealth, *and* protect you from taxes.** Which strategy sounds better to you?

Term

"Buy Term and Invest the Difference."

The revolt against WL insurance came about in the 1970s with the rise in popularity of "Buy Term and Invest the Difference." This philosophy actually made sense, in theory. It was:

- You should purchase an inexpensive term insurance policy to cover the 20 or 30 years when you have more dependents/responsibilities, such as children and a mortgage, and invest the remaining amount you have saved by not purchasing "expensive" permanent life insurance.

- Then invest the difference/savings within a Roth IRA in the stock market for retirement.

These advisors will tell you, *"When your term expires, your investments will have grown large enough that you will no longer need to work anymore. You will have become 'self-insured,' and you won't need life insurance in your retirement years."*

Is that an accurate statement?

Yes, **in theory** this philosophy works. But it has more failures than successes.

The **first flaw** with this philosophy is that the average investor only earns around **4.1%** return long-term on their stock market investments. At that rate, those investments will never grow enough to retire. Not even close. (see Dalbar study on page 28)

The **second flaw** in this philosophy comes about when you ask this question: "What do I do when my term insurance expires in 20 or 30 years, and I may not be able to afford the huge premiums to extend the coverage?" Or worse, "What if I become uninsurable?"

The **third flaw** with this philosophy is that it doesn't solve the problem of providing affordable long-term care (LTC) insurance to protect the assets you have accumulated. Most Americans when they retire find that the cost of LTC is simply not affordable, or they have become uninsurable, and can't qualify for LTC coverage.

The **fourth flaw** with this philosophy is that statistically most Americans (and Canadians) are horrible savers. Most people only save when they are forced to do so. Many do actually buy the term insurance, but very few actually follow through to fund a Roth IRA. In my opinion, this strategy should be renamed "Buy term and forget the difference."

We will cover the importance of **forced savings** later in this book.

The **final flaw** in this philosophy is the limitation on annual funding of Roth IRAs, currently $6000 a year, and $7000 a year if over age 50. This amount of investing is just too small to build wealth.

If you refer back to Chapter 2 (Roth IRA) of *Top 10 Ways to Avoid Taxes* to the Story of the Four Brothers, you may recall that Danny, after 40 years of investing in the market, had accumulated $2,675,000 in his Roth IRA for his retirement. That would provide an income of about $160,000 a year.

But when making adjustments for inflation, "Danny would be retiring on about $40,000 a year in today's dollars." But *that* was also assuming an average of 10% rate of return over that 40-year period.

If Danny had only earned 5% return on his Roth IRA, this would provide about $10,000 a year of income during his retirement.

Do you remember my investment philosophy regarding investing?

"If I can't use Other People's Money (OPM), it is not a good investment. PERIOD. No exceptions."

For this reason alone, I don't use Roth IRAs in my investing.

Universal Life (UL)

UL sales boomed in the late **1970s** and **1980's** for one reason: Interest rates skyrocketed in response to out-of-control inflation rates.

Bank savings accounts were paying 13%+, and it made sense to essentially put a bank account into a life insurance policy, and **earn 13%+ return, tax-free and risk free**.

This philosophy worked great, but when interest rates fell in the late 80s, 90s and continued to fall up to now, this philosophy also fell apart. With interest rates this low, both returns on UL and WL are at historical lows.

Bank Prime Loan Rate – 1960-2020

Variable Universal Life (VUL)

VUL became popular in the stock market boom of the **1990s.**

This philosophy was simple:

Put mutual funds called "subaccounts" into an insurance policy. Once sheltered under IRC 7702a, you would be exempt from the taxes on all the gains, including your dividends from stocks and bonds.

This works great when the stock markets are rising! But when stocks fall, FEAR becomes a factor once again, and the average investor produces very poor results.

Because VULs *can* lose money, as opposed to IULs, the insurance companies will not lend money secured by the cash value inside the insurance policy.

This means there are no options for investing with OPM with a VUL.

Once again, this goes against my #1 rule for investing.

Indexed Universal Life (IUL)

The first IUL was created in 1997. This came about when some genius at an insurance company took a risk-free investment, called a "Market-Linked CD," and put it inside an insurance policy. Once sheltered under IRC 7702a, the gains would be exempt from all taxes.

Market Linked CDs had **5 distinct advantages** from investing in the markets:

1. The investments would rise based on the performance of an Index, such as the S&P 500.

2. They had an annual cap to the earnings, such as 10%.

3. The gains would lock-in annually,

4. They had a floor of 0%, where the investments wouldn't participate in any losses when the Index would decline,

5. The investments would begin to grow in value when the markets began to recover, even if the market never exceeded the previous highs. (Please note the following illustration. As they say, "a picture is worth a thousand words.")

And Voila, IUL was born! And with it, tax-free, and risk-free investing!

(Although by law, IULs are not considered "investments" and are regulated under insurance tax codes.)

So... now I'm going to attempt to guess your next question:

"Mark, how effective is the IUL for growing money in the market, in both market-booms, market-crashes, and when the market recovers?"

We'll take a look at the same 20-year period we covered earlier in this book and compare. If you recall, the S&P 500 was at around 1500 in March of 2000, and **briefly** rose just above 3000 at the end of 2019. It took **two decades** to double in value. That is an average compounded rate of return of only **3.6%**! (If you include dividends, the return is increased to about 6.72%.[1])

Let's illustrate the power of not losing money. First, we'll look at this comparison:

A. If you had invested $1,000 in the S&P 500 and let it ride through the ups and down of the market, vs

---

[1] https://www.officialdata.org/us/stocks/s-p-500/2000?amount=100&endYear=2019

B. If you had invested $1,000 with a **floor of 0%**, where you could not lose money, but you **capped the gains to just 10%**.

First, let's look at a floor of zero, and a cap of 10%.

Year	% Return	$1,000.00	% Return	$1,000.00
		S&P 500		**0% - 10%**
2000	-10.14%	$898.60	0.00%	$1,000.00
2001	-13.04%	$781.42	0.00%	$1,000.00
2002	-23.37%	$598.80	0.00%	$1,000.00
2003	26.38%	$756.77	10.00%	$1,100.00
2004	8.99%	$824.80	8.99%	$1,198.89
2005	3.00%	$849.55	3.00%	$1,234.86
2006	13.62%	$965.25	10.00%	$1,358.34
2007	3.53%	$999.33	3.53%	$1,406.29
2008	-38.49%	$614.69	0.00%	$1,406.29
2009	23.45%	$758.83	10.00%	$1,546.92
2010	12.78%	$855.81	10.00%	$1,701.61
2011	0.00%	$855.81	0.00%	$1,701.61
2012	13.41%	$970.57	10.00%	$1,871.77
2013	29.60%	$1,257.86	10.00%	$2,058.95
2014	11.39%	$1,401.13	10.00%	$2,264.85
2015	-0.73%	$1,390.91	0.00%	$2,264.85
2016	9.54%	$1,523.60	9.54%	$2,480.91
2017	19.42%	$1,819.48	10.00%	$2,729.00
2018	-6.24%	$1,705.94	0.00%	$2,729.00
2019	28.88%	**$2,198.62**	10.00%	**$3,001.91**

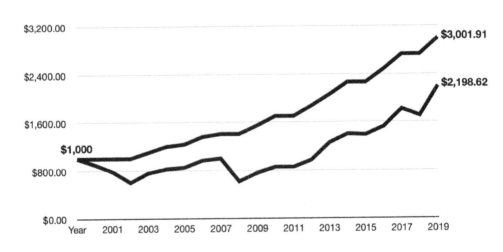

As you can see, the $1,000 in the S&P 500 at the end of the 20-year period with booms and bust would grow to **$2,198**. This doesn't include any dividends, but is also excluding the most recent crash.

The same $1,000 would grow to **$3,001**, if you added a floor, and a cap of 10%!

Would you like to see a **floor of 0%**, and a **cap of 15%**?

Let's see the results of raising the cap by just 5%.

Next page...

ir	% Return	S&P 500 $1,000.00	% Return	0% - 15% $1,000.00
2000	-10.14%	$898.60	0.00%	$1,000.00
2001	-13.04%	$781.42	0.00%	$1,000.00
2002	-23.37%	$598.80	0.00%	$1,000.00
2003	26.38%	$756.77	15.00%	$1,150.00
2004	8.99%	$824.80	8.99%	$1,253.39
2005	3.00%	$849.55	3.00%	$1,290.99
2006	13.62%	$965.25	13.62%	$1,466.82
2007	3.53%	$999.33	3.53%	$1,518.60
2008	-38.49%	$614.69	0.00%	$1,518.60
2009	23.45%	$758.83	15.00%	$1,746.39
2010	12.78%	$855.81	12.78%	$1,969.58
2011	0.00%	$855.81	0.00%	$1,969.58
2012	13.41%	$970.57	13.41%	$2,233.70
2013	29.60%	$1,257.86	15.00%	$2,568.75
2014	11.39%	$1,401.13	11.39%	$2,861.33
2015	-0.73%	$1,390.91	0.00%	$2,861.33
2016	9.54%	$1,523.60	9.54%	$3,134.30
2017	19.42%	$1,819.48	15.00%	$3,604.45
2018	-6.24%	$1,705.94	0.00%	$3,604.45
2019	28.88%	$2,198.62	15.00%	$4,145.11

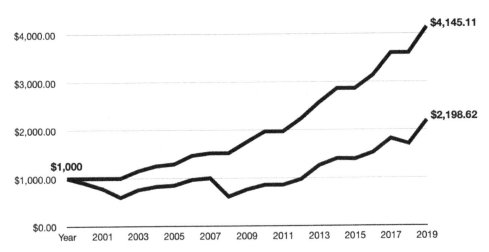

Yup, just by raising the cap by 5%, the performance of $1,000 grows to over **$4,145**!

(Note: These figures are for illustration purposes only, and purposely exclude capital gains tax and insurance costs.)

I can hear the IUL skeptics already.

"What about the fees?"

Yes, it is true we are not showing "the fees and charges" of an IUL in the above illustrations. We are only trying to demonstrate the power of not losing money in a market downturn.

We are also not showing the "fees" and realities of investing in the market. Is it all about the fees?

The Fear Penalty

This is different for everyone, but it is a fact that most of the investors don't earn the average rate of return of the market, especially over 20 years with multiple major downturns. I refer to this as "the fear penalty" as it has a far bigger reduction to growth than "the fees."

In fact, a study by Dalbar, Inc., a company which studies investor behavior and analyzes investor returns, consistently shows that the average stock market investor earns below-average returns.

They found that when the market averaged 10% return over a 30-year period, investors are earning less than half of the market, **about 4.1%.**

And this is for investors that intended to fully participate in the market—without reducing their exposure by blending their portfolio with bonds.

The fear penalty comes into play when asked on an investment survey:

"Are you low, low/medium, medium,
medium/high or a high-risk investor?"

Or

"If you took a 30% loss in your portfolio, would you be concerned?"

Because these are "scary questions" for many, many investors end up in a 60%/40% (stock/bond), or a 70%/30% (stock/bond) portfolio. These investors also never get the average returns of the market.

When Dalbar reviewed the average bond mutual fund investor over the same 30-year period, they averaged just **0.26%**!

Many of these well-intentioned investors added bonds to their portfolios to reduce the "risk" of stocks. Their result was that their investments didn't even keep ahead of inflation.

Oh Yes, The Fees!

There are also the fees that will be deducted for management of many mutual funds, most of which perform worse than an index fund. Then they deduct their fees. An extra 1% fee compounded over 20 years adds up to a very large reduction in growth.

For example, if growing $1,000 over 20 years at 6% rate of return, the portfolio grows to $3,310. Deduct a 1% annual management fee, it only grows to about **$2,712**. That is 18% less growth. But there are more deductions to come…

Taxes on the Growth!

We are not factoring in that many of these investment accounts are non-retirement accounts, and taxes must be paid as they grow. The stated returns of the market are not accounting for deducting the taxes from those stated returns.

The returns to investors over 20 years are drastically reduced when accounting for the 20%, or 30% (could be more or less) capital gains taxes upon the sale. If you take the **$2,712** number from above, and deduct the $1000 contributed, you have gains of **$1,712**. If you deduct 25% for state and federal taxes, you are left with **$1,284**, which is now your after-tax profit.

And we did not yet deduct the taxes on the dividends received each year over 20 years. Since dividends are taxed at the highest rates, this cuts even further into your return.

Taxes at Retirement

Most importantly, if investing in a traditional IRA or 401(k), the gains will grow tax-free, but are fully taxable at the highest tax rate when taking distribution in retirement. The bigger the gains, the bigger share the government can take!

That is a big "fee" of 30% to 50% of your income…taken annually at retirement, year after year, for the rest of your life. And, you can pass down the ongoing taxes to your heirs when they inherit what remains of your IRA, so they too can pay taxes annually, year after year…for the rest of their lives.

Loss of Sleep

During 24, and 15 months of market crashes (see "The Peak," pages 12 and 13), when fear is highest, how many investors are losing sleep? Is sleep also important to you?

The Divorce Penalty

Many people experience this "penalty" when having money problems.

And, losing large amounts of money in the stock market has been proven to cause stress, depression, loss of sleep, arguments with loved ones, which are all big factors for causing divorce. In fact, money is ranked #1 for "the causes of divorce."

How big is this large penalty? Potentially, **50% of everything you own?**

Life Insurance and Long-Term Care Costs

Let's keep in mind that the investors in the stock market will still need to purchase long-term care insurance for asset protection, and most would like to have life insurance after their term insurance expires.

So even the investor that does earn the full historical rate of 10% will still need to pay the cost of buying permanent life insurance and LTC outside of their stock market investing.

And Finally, the Coronavirus Crash!

As we mentioned, we are not showing the latest crash of the market as we don't know where the bottom will be. Or how long the market will take to recover to the previous high.

Now, let's get back to IUL.

Let me give you the good news about the most recent upgrades to IULs, even *after* I released "Top 10 Ways to Avoid Taxes" in late 2018.

I refer to them as the "Next Generation of IULs."

- As I mentioned in Top "10 Ways to Avoid Taxes," there have been no cap strategies as an investment option for many years, but only in a handful of IULs. This can be a powerful strategy to use, specifically when coming out of a recession, or after a bear market (defined as a -20% decline or more). But now it is possible to "supercharge" your IUL for even greater returns. When utilizing this strategy, it is possible to net a 20% return on your cash value, if the S&P 500 returns just 11% rate of return that year.

• Today, we are seeing IULs with caps of 20%.

• IULs even exist where you can participate in the upside potential of all three major indexes: NASDAQ 100, S&P 500 and the Dow Jones, where you get 50% of your account credited to the monthly average of whichever index performs the best, 30% to the next best, and 20% to the least.

Yes, this sounds more like sorcery rather than investing.

But the companies that developed these strategies are household names, with roots dating back 100 to 150 years, or more!

Note: In order for an IUL to have higher caps, or to "supercharge" the potential upside, options contracts are purchased. It is possible to pay a fee of 1%, or up to 7.5% of your cash value, which is used to purchase "call" options on the indexes. Buying these options can potentially earn much higher rates of returns than the market, and even double the returns after paying for the fee. In the years where the market goes down, this could be a 1% - 7.5% loss of the cash value.

PART TWO:
21 WAYS TO BUILD IT!

Lifetime Financial Planning

1. Financial Indepedence vs. "Retirement"

Most define retirement as the day when they no longer have to go to work. For most, it is generally age 65 or 70.

They only get to retire if:

- They invest properly throughout their entire lives,
- Earn a consistently good rate of return,
- Eliminate debt and future bills/payments,
- Plan properly for tax reduction/avoidance,
- Plan properly for asset protection,
- And earn high enough rates of return during their 30+ years of retirement...so they don't run out of money.

Statistically, the odds of this happening are incredibly small.

If the above does not sound exciting to you, and maybe even a little scary, simply change your goal.

In my opinion, **financial independence** should be your goal, not "retirement." Financial independence has nothing to do with age.

Financial independence for me is defined as:

When your passive income exceeds your expenses and you no longer have to work. You may "work" when you want, and only on the things that you enjoy.

If you are a reader that is in your 20s or 30s, my hope is that you become financially independent long before age 60 or 65. To do so, you will need to use investment strategies that generate tax-free income/profit that can be accessed long before the typical retirement age.

You may also want to simultaneously fund tax-free strategies that can be accessed after retirement age.

As you may have read about in Chapter 6 of Top 10 Ways to Avoid Taxes, similar to a Roth IRA, insurance policies must be funded with after-tax money.

The money grows without taxes and can be accessed at any age with no taxes or penalties. One opportunity, after a market decline (or a crash) is to borrow from your IUL, which didn't lose money, and fund (or add money to) a Roth IRA when stock prices have declined. This strategy is effective to buy more shares of stock when shares are "on sale."

Here is my favorite part about this strategy:

If funding a Roth IRA with tax-free gains from your IUL, you funded a tax-free Roth IRA, with tax-free profits from your IUL. **That's double tax-free!**

Remember, since the profits from an IUL can be accessed at any age, they can be accessed for investing outside of your IUL, whenever you see an opportunity.

IUL profits can be accessed tax-free prior to age 60, and your Roth IRA can be accessed tax-free after age 60.

Finally, at retirement age, since both IUL and Roth IRAs don't trigger taxation on your social security payments (Google "Provisional Income"), you can access:

- Tax-free income from your Roth IRA,
- Tax-free income from your IUL,
- And, tax-free income from your social security.
- **That's three income streams, all tax-free!**

Note: This is assuming that distributions from any tax-deferred retirement accounts, such as IRAs or 401(k)s, don't trigger taxes on your social security benefits.

2. Use a Term/IUL Combination

Remember, the **purpose of term insurance** is inexpensive life insurance coverage for a period of time, perhaps 10, 20, or 30 years. If you pass away during the term, the death benefit is paid to your family.

After that term, the insurance expires, or the rates become too expensive for most to afford. There is no additional benefit.

Term is generally used when you have larger responsibilities, such as children, a mortgage or other debt, and perhaps future education costs. Term can give you a large amount of life insurance, for a relatively small amount of money. It should be purchased when you are in good health.

The **purpose of an IUL** is very different. The basic benefits are:

- Permanent Life insurance
- Growth of cash value
- Protection from market declines

- Protection from taxes
- Long-term care for asset protection

To reduce costs, you will want to buy a large portion of your insurance as term, and you should be certain your term can be converted to IUL later, if desired.

The first step is to figure out how much life insurance you need overall. Then calculate how much should be term, and how much should be IUL. To calculate the total amount of coverage needed, use the "**DIME**" formula. D.I.M.E. is an acronym for:

Debt, Income, Mortgage, Education
DEBT

Add up your total debt, for example:

$40,000   in auto loans and credit cards.
$60,000   in student loans.
$100,000

INCOME

Then take your annual earned income and multiply it by 10.

$80,000   a year
x 10
$800,000

MORTGAGE

Then add your mortgage balance. Let's assume it is:

$500,000

EDUCATION

Finally, what will the cost of college be for the kids? Let's say that number is:

$250,000 (Yes, this could be dramatically more or less.)

Your total amount of insurance needed would be:

$100,000
$800,000
$500,000
$250,000

$1,650,000   **of total coverage needed**

As I mentioned, term is the least expensive type of insurance, *but not all term is the same.*

Convertible vs Non-Convertible Term

Convertible simply means that you can "convert" your term insurance (which expires) into permanent life insurance (IUL is my personal favorite type) which doesn't have an expiration date.

This feature is invaluable if someone were to have a change in health and become uninsurable, like I did.

Some term policies are not convertible from the day that you buy them. Some are only convertible for a few years, perhaps 5 or 10 years.

Non-convertible term is the worst type of term insurance, as the insurance company knows that the majority of term insurance policies will expire worthless...meaning they don't ever have to pay a claim. For example:

- Let's say at age 35 you purchased a 20-year term policy (expires at age 55), and you developed health issues at age 54, but didn't pass away until at age 59. The premiums you paid for 20 years will be gone, and the life insurance company will not pay a dime to your family.

- Alternatively, if you purchased a fully convertible 20-year term policy, and you developed health issues at 54, and wanted to ensure you passed a death benefit to your heirs, you could convert your term policy to a permanent IUL, regardless of health.

- As long as you properly funded the IUL, the full death benefit would pass to your heirs. And the 20 years of funding your inexpensive term would not have gone to waste.

You should always ask:

Is this term convertible?
For how long?
If convertible, what can I convert it into?
Is IUL an option?

What about costs?

Here are approximate numbers for convertible term insurance:

- A 35-year-old, healthy male could purchase a 30-year term of $1,250,000 for about $86 a month.

- A 35-year-old healthy female could purchase a 30-year term of $1,250,000 for about $72 a month.

So, let's get back to our scenario above when calculating how much insurance should be term, and how much should be IUL.

If you needed a total of $1,650,000 of life insurance, and purchased convertible term of $1,250,000, your remaining life insurance coverage needed is $400,000. This could be purchased as an IUL to provide:

- Permanent life insurance, for when your term expires,
- Long-term care if you should become very sick,
- Tax-free, and risk-free investing,
- All the others benefits of an IUL,
- And my favorite…**Build a Tax-Free Family Bank**! (we will be covering this one shortly!)

3. Inexpensive Long-Term Care (LTC) Insurance

LTC coverage is valuable for asset protection. The topic of LTC could be a book on its own, citing the statistics, costs etc., but for the sake of this book, it is important to know that many Americans will be forced to spend-down all their assets, their savings, 401(k)s, and the equity in their home to pay for the costs of care when they get older. Many couples leave their spouse in very difficult financial shape (statistically, it's most commonly women), because they don't factor in the costs for LTC into their financial calculations in retirement.

Stand-alone LTC coverage, purchased as a single benefit, historically can be very expensive. But, by adding it on as a "rider" to permanent life insurance, such as an IUL, it can drastically reduce the costs for that protection.

For the sake of this book, we want to highlight the inherent benefits with regards to LTC in the next generation of IULs:

First, the cost of LTC coverage is much cheaper than stand-alone coverage, because it is being paid for out of the death benefit of your life insurance policy. This reduces risk to the insurance company, and therefore reduces your costs too. You can think of this as having long-term care if you need it, but if you don't use it, it passes to your heirs tax-free as a death benefit. It is not a "use it or lose it" scenario like with many stand-alone LTC policies.

Second, when applying for life insurance with an LTC rider, they will assess both risk of death (life insurance coverage) and morbidity risk, which is your level of health and wellness (LTC coverage). Once approved for both, you will have the benefits of life insurance and LTC paid out of the death benefit.

For example, if a spouse/loved one needs care in their home for two years, the death benefit will be liquidated for that time to provide the income needed for that care. At death, the remaining unused death benefit, plus the cash value, will pass on to the spouse/family tax-free.

What is interesting about LTC is it is not just used by the elderly. Statistics show that 40% of people that use LTC are between the ages of 18 and 65. So by having an IUL with an LTC rider, at any point in your life if you needed LTC, you can use the cash value in your IUL to pay for those needs, and/or liquidate some of the death benefit, without having to liquidate any other assets to do so.

Third, generally, life insurance and LTC premiums must be paid for with **after-tax dollars**. But the **growth** of the cash value inside of an IUL is not taxable. And when funded properly, that tax-free growth could begin to pay for your life insurance and LTC premiums!

I was curious…

I am almost 43 years old and was wondering how much the cost of this LTC rider would be, assuming I could get the best health rating. When running a quick quote, the cost for the rider on a $500,000 life insurance policy was $246 a year.

Yes, that is about **$20 a month** for $500,000 of LTC coverage! To learn more facts about LTC, I'm including here a report, "Will the Myths of Long Term Care Leave You Unprotected." (See next page.)?

Will the Myths of Long Term Care Leave You Unprotected?

Long-term care (LTC) is a subject that people don't like to think about. A lot of myths exist—myths like, "Long term care means going to a nursing home." It helps to be educated on what long-term care really means to **you.** And learning what the reality is can help you make the right decision for yourself or your parents.

Myth 1. LTC will be paid for by health insurance, Medicare or Medicaid.

Reality: Health insurance only pays for people who are going to get better. Medicare only pays a maximum of 100 days coverage after a 3 consecutive day stay in a nursing home, and only the first 20 days are free. Medicaid is for the impoverished, which means assets have to be less than $2,000.

Myth 2. "Most people who need LTC go to a nursing home."

Reality: Most long-term care is given outside a nursing home. Statistics show 73% of people who need LTC live and are able to receive care at home or in a community service setting (assisted living, adult day care etc.)1.

Myth 3. "My parents and grandparents did not need LTC, so neither will I."

Reality: There is a 50% chance you will need some type of long-term care2.
If you live to the age of 65, there is a 70% chance you will need LTC.

Myth 4. "My spouse and I can just take care of each other."

Reality: Women who live past age 65 have a 50% greater chance of entering a nursing home than a man1.
Women need care longer (on average 3.5 years) than do men (on average 2.2 years).4
On average women live 5 years longer than a man1.

Myth 5. "Long-term care is for old people."

Reality: Approximately 40% of individuals who require LTC are age 18 and 64.4

Myth 6. I'll just pay for long-term care out of savings.

Reality: The average stay in a nursing home is 2.5 years, and the average time in care outside a nursing home is 4.5 years.
The average annual cost of a private room in a nursing home is $87,235 and a semi-private room is $78,110. Assisted Living averages $41,724 per year.
Specialized home health care averages a cost of $21 per hour.

1. The 2011 Sourcebook for Long-term Care Insurance Information - American Association for Long-Term Care Insurance 2011
2. "What are the Chances of Needing Long-term Care?" June 2010
3. 2011 Medicare Handbook (www.medicare.gov)
4. U.S. Dept. Of Health & Human Services, National Underwriter Life and Health - "Riding the Life Extension Wave," Nov.11, 2011
5. "What is Long-Term Care? The Misunderstood Health Care," www.guidetolongtermcare.com (2010)
6. Mature Market Institute, Markel Survey of Long-term Care Costs, October 2011

4. Cash Value Rises With the Stock Market, Never Falls!

We covered this previously in this book, but to summarize:

Your cash value inside an IUL will grow when the market rises.

It is possible in the Next Generation of IULs to earn returns higher than the market. And, YOU CAN'T LOSE MONEY.

5. Fear/Emotion Management

We touched upon the **fear penalty** earlier in this book.

Management of emotions, including fear, greed, discouragement, excitement, and *fear of missing out*, or "**FOMO**" is key to successful investing.

And, as we covered briefly before, despite the experts telling you to dollar cost average (meaning consistently buy regardless if markets are going up or down), it is safe to say that when markets are volatile—rising quickly, or crashing—emotions take control, and many investors respond in 4 ways:

1. They buy when the market is rising for extended periods of time and there is lots of good news (They experience **optimism**, and/or **FOMO**).

2. They sell when the markets are crashing, especially when suffering long market declines over 12 months (**fear**).

3. Once sold, they lock-in their losses (feeling **discouraged**) and many won't buy back in even when stocks may be "on sale." They wait until the markets look **safe** again…and are having a long-term upward trend. (They repeat #1)

4. Many don't happen to buy in again at all, and if they do, they invest too conservatively (**because of fear of loss**) never earning the true gains of the stock market.

Yes, all the smartest investing books and talking heads warn to not do the above, but the vast majority of people do so with their 401(k), IRAs, and stock market investments. They do this over and over, again and again. Once **FEAR** takes control, investment results are less than half that of the market.

This also explains why Americans have over 11 TRILLION dollars sitting idle in bank accounts and money markets, earning virtually nothing.

Conversely, how do emotions affect the returns when investing inside an IUL?

1. When the markets are rising, you can buy **without ever worrying** "when is the next crash coming?" Who cares?

2. During downturns or a crash you won't lose money, so there is **no fear, and no need to sell**. In fact, I've found that clients who own IULs feel excited they are not losing any money, when their other retirement accounts and mutual funds are.

3. Buying in a downturn with an IUL is **fun and exciting**, because while no one knows how long it will continue to go down, each time you are investing more, you are in fact "buying low," without the risk of losing if the market continues to decline.

4. When the markets start to recover, your potential of total growth is even higher. **That's exciting** because your principal hasn't decreased during the downturn. With an IUL you remove the fear. And...

The bigger the crash the better
your results can be over the long-term!

You are very happy to buy, again and again, month after month. It doesn't matter if fear is high, and stocks are crashing, or if markets are rising, and there is eventually a market crash. It is important to understand that not properly managing your emotions when investing can dramatically affect your returns.

6. Forced Savings

Statistically, most people save almost all their money in three places:

5. Their home (generally appreciates in value)

6. Their cars (generally depreciating in value, and the worst "investment")

7. Their 401(k) (appreciating… and sometimes depreciating)

All have one common theme: forced savings.

IULs have also been proven to be effective for "forced savings" by treating the funding of an IUL like a bill – similar to your mortgage, car payment, or retirement account.

But keep in mind that an IUL separates itself from your other investments with one key benefit: **It is the only one of the three that can ONLY go up in value!**

And because IULs can only go up, this is a great place to access cash. The loans, secured by the cash value can be used to buy more real estate when prices are down, invest in a business or other opportunity, or even add more money to retirement accounts or other investment accounts, after a market crash when the stocks are considered "cheap" or "on sale."

7. Annual Lock-Ins or Every Two-to-Five Years (It's Up to You!)

In the past, the gains of an IUL would "lock-in" annually.

But today, you have the option of locking-in gains every two-to-five years for a higher cap.

For example, an IUL on the market may have a cap of 25% based on the 2-year performance of the S&P 500. Although it is not common for the S&P 500 to earn 25% in one year, it is quite common to earn 25% over two years—which can be safely locked-in with no chance of losing your gains in the future.

For example, if you purchased into this strategy at the start of 2018, the returns of the market were:

-6.24%	2018
28.88%	2019

You would lock-in gains of about **22%**, and could not lose those gains in 2020, regardless of the outcome of coronavirus.

8. No Cap Strategies

For a fee, you can remove the cap to the gains you can earn each year based on the performance of the S&P 500. You won't have a cap, but the cost (or fee) is you cannot participate in the first 5% of the gains. Let's look at the same example above of the S&P 500:

-6.24%	2018
28.88%	2019

That first year would not take a loss. Good News! The second year, when the market earned 28.88%, you would not participate in the first 5% of the gains (there is cost for protecting you against loss). But… there would be no cap to your growth. At the end of the year, your cash value would be credited a return of **+23.88%.**

And…if you happen to have added a large amount of money to your IUL at the start of 2020, and shortly after the market began to crash, and the fear index hits 85, you may find yourself cool, calm, collected…and sleeping like a baby.

9. No Taxes During Growth

Yup, no state, federal or capital gains taxes during the growth of your money…for the rest of your life!

10. No Maximum Annual Contributions

Yes, that's right! There are no limits to the contributions you can make to an IUL. It is only limited by the size of the death benefit. Your age and gender are also a factor. Unlike IRAs, SEP IRAs, 401(k)s, Roth IRAs, or most standard retirement accounts, the IUL gives you complete flexibility in designing how much you'd like to save each year. Whether you just have an extra $10,000 a year you'd like to set aside, or $100,000 a month.

11. No Age Restrictions, or Requirements

The one downside of an IUL is that it does have health requirements to qualify.

But there are **no age restrictions** or **requirements** like there are with traditional retirement accounts.

As you may be aware, retirement accounts generally **restrict** access to your money prior to age 59 ½ or a 10% penalty will apply, plus the taxes.

The money in your IUL can be accessed at any age for any purpose.

Invest! Buy real estate! Fund college! Or… buy a new Supercar! There are no restrictions to accessing your cash, based on your age, no penalties will apply, and… no taxes!

Because the government wants your money in your retirement accounts, they **require** that you start depleting your accounts (to pay taxes) at age 72 (previously 70½ before the CARES Act) called required minimum distributions, or "RMDs."

Similar to a Roth IRA, there are no RMDs for IULs.

(Yes, as I'm writing this book, the 10% penalty for IRA withdrawals prior to age 59 1/2 has been waived, but it doesn't waive the taxes. The good news is the taxes can be spread over three years. And, if you pay that amount back to your account within the three years you can also avoid the taxes.)

12. No Income Restrictions

Retirement accounts such as Roth IRAs can be funded as long as your income doesn't rise above a certain amount, such as $139,000 for a single person in 2019.

IULs have no such income restrictions.

So, if you happen to be reading this and you are a "**HENRY**" a High Earner Not Rich Yet, you may find yourself restricted to funding Roth IRAs and other retirement accounts, and what will you do with all that cash after Uncle Sam takes his share?

Here is the good news: IULs don't have income restrictions whatsoever.

So HENRYS, and Rich People, and ultra-high net worth (UHNW) folks can all benefit from an IUL.

13. "Rollover Minutes"

In traditional retirements accounts, you have annual contribution restrictions, such as $6000 to Roth IRA, or $19,500 to your 401(k), or "X amount" to your SEP IRA. If you miss a year, the IRS doesn't allow you to catch up and add the amount you did not contribute the previous year.

Within an IUL you can always catchup from the years you didn't make the maximum annual contribution. For example, let's say you were able to save as much as $20,000 each year into your IUL, but only funded $10,000 one year. You could add $30,000 the next year… without violating IRC 7702a.

I like to think of this as having "Rollover Minutes." Do you remember the cell phone commercials? (Those under a certain age have no idea what I'm talking about, lol.)

Beat the Big Banks

14. Build a Tax-Free Family Bank!

Okay, I'll try not to go on a tangent about banks for too long!

If you want to know what I concluded when researching the "alternatives to saving in the banks," you can read my first book, *Rich Man Poor Bank*. What that book demonstrates is: "What the banks don't want you to know about money."

I believe the most important lesson in the book is that it reveals the **inverse relationship** between bank profit and financial literacy. In other words, *the higher a person's financial education, the less money the banks will earn from them during their life.*

Financial Education ▼ = Bank Profit ▲

Financial Education ▲ = Bank Profit ▼

And since these publicly traded megabanks have one primary goal – "Maximizing profit for their shareholders" – it is imperative that the banks must keep Americans financially illiterate to ensure they maximize their profit. The banks' mantra, which has not changed during my lifetime, is:

> *"Saving money and getting good credit will lead to your financial security."*

I concluded something quite different:

> *"Saving money and getting good credit makes bankers wealthy!"*

Let's illustrate one of the most important lessons in "Rich Man Poor Bank," specifically, the "RULE OF 72." The rule of 72 calculates how long it will take for your money to double when earning a particular rate of interest:

Simply divide the rate you are earning into the number 72.

For example, if earning 1% on a savings account, divide 1 into 72 and you will get the number 72. So "72" is the amount of years it will take for your money to double when earning 1% return on bank savings.

How about if your bank is not paying 1%, rather is paying you 0.1%? Take out your calculator and you will find it takes 720 years for your money to double.

At .02% it takes 3,600 years to double your money.

The same rule also applies for how long it takes for debt to double. For example, many Americans carry credit card debt at 16% - 24%.

At 16%, credit card debt doubles every 4 ¼ years.

At 24%, credit card debt doubles every 3 years.

What is most important to understand is that the banks judge your credit worthiness based on your credit score. The higher the score, the less risk and the better rates you can get. The lower the score, the more risk, and the rates will be higher.

This model ensures that when you need it most, perhaps when you lost a job and find yourself in financial hot water, the banks will hammer you the hardest, with the highest interest rates… as you are not credit worthy without a job. And, when you have a job and are doing well financially and don't need the money, the banks are happy to lend it to you, again, only when you don't really need it.

At the same time, the "financial gurus" and talking heads on TV recommend:

> *"Keep six-to-twelve months of savings in your*
> *bank account for emergency funds."*

And the megabanks are happy to help you save it — resulting in 11 billion+ in bank savings, CDs and money market accounts. The banks are happy to comply and put that money hard to work *for them*.

What is important to understand is that these "rules" were built specifically by the banks, for the benefit of the banks, and to enrich only the banks.

How about you create your own rules?

How about having the ability to borrow at the lowest rates, regardless of your credit score, or even if you don't have a job or income?

What if you never again needed to *"keep six-to-twelve months of savings in your bank account for emergency funds"* and your money was working hard for you rather than the banks?

As we covered earlier in this book, the funds in an IUL grow free of state, federal and capital gains taxes. You can access these funds with no penalties, no income, no age restrictions, and no taxes.

There are certain IULs that even allow you to use the cash value as collateral, and you can give yourself a tax-free loan against it, while keeping the full amount of funds "invested" and growing inside the IUL.

For example, if you had $200,000 of cash value in your IUL and you wanted to borrow $100,000 to purchase an investment property or put towards a business – really, you can use it for anything you want – you can take a loan of that $100,000 (no taxes on loans) while still having the full $200,000 to grow in the market, tax-free and risk-free!

Yes, it is like your IUL becomes your own personal Tax-Free Family Bank!

I'm assuming you remember my #1 Rule for Investing?

Here is how I personally structure my finances…so the mega-banks don't get to use my money, and I can use OPM in all my investing:

For Banking:

I use a credit union as they are not-for-profit. They have members (you) rather than shareholders, so they don't have the goal of maximizing shareholder value. Both my checking account and my business account are held at the local credit union. I don't pay fees for either.

I have a credit card from my credit union that is around 9% interest. And most importantly, I can take a cash from this card with no fees, and they will lend it to me at the 9% interest rate even on a cash advance. This is a different from a bank-issued credit card which would first charge a 5% cash advance fee, plus 24% annual interest, or more.

Let's illustrate the difference in costs if I needed to borrow, let's say $10,000 in a bind. And I only want to borrow for a month and didn't want to liquidate any investments to do so.

At my credit union, I would simply logon to the credit union App and transfer the $10,000 from my credit card into my checking account. Again, no fees would apply.

My megabank-issued card would **first** charge a cash advance fee of 5%, or $500.

Then they would begin charging 24% interest on the amount borrowed.

For one month, that would be about 2%, or $200.

My credit union would charge 9% annually, so for one month that is about 0.75%, or $75.

Total bank fees and interest when borrowing $10,000 for one month:

      If borrowing from a megabank = **$700**
      If borrowing from my credit union = **$75**

Because of this "backup emergency fund," I save very little in the credit union, I don't have anything in my savings account, and keep most of my money invested in other places working hard for me.

I also have a megabank-issued credit card I use for my business. I charge it up for business expenses and pay it down to zero each month, so I also pay zero in interest. I earn the airmiles/perks and money back, so the megabank pays me to use their money.

Thanks, credit union! And thanks, bank!

      My financial education ▲ = Bank Profit ▼

For Investing:

I have a brokerage account and I can invest in municipal bond ETFs and receive tax-free dividends. (I can also buy other ETFs, stocks, etc.)

I also am approved for "margin" which gives me the ability to borrow at super low interest rates for additional investing, with no credit check and no income verification. The current rate to borrow on margin is **2.55%.**

So, my money is always working hard for me, earns tax-free dividends, and is fully liquid. That is another source for emergency funds if I ever need it.

For Insurance:

I have a large 30-year convertible term insurance policy to keep my life insurance costs down as much as possible.

I have a "next generation IUL" with an LTC rider, and a 20% cap, and the ability to borrow at low interest rates, if needed... and with no credit check or income verification.

It is possible to have many years of reserves growing without risk and taxes, so that you too can weather the storm in any economy.

As you can see, I have the option to use OPM in all my investing when I see an opportunity, and I don't need to apply with a banker if I want to borrow. I can borrow for any reason at all.

To summarize:

I have good credit, but don't need it to borrow. And I don't listen to the talking heads on TV, and "Keep six-to-twelve months of savings in my bank account for emergency funds."

College & Education

15. College Funding

College for me was a fun experience. The beer, the pub crawls, the bar hopping, the girls, and brewing even more beer during the three hours of free time between classes (yes, we love beer in Canada).

I was pretty broke. And working at the ice cream factory during the summer making (and eating) the Häagen Dazs 500ml Vanilla Swiss Almond ice cream really helped reduce the cost of buying food, which of course left me more money for beer. I'm sure glad I had a super-metabolism with all that beer and ice cream. This was 20+ years ago.

I thought for sure the business class would teach me business skills, and how to make my millions. I ended up dropping out after a couple of years and walked away with $25,000+ in student loans and credit card debts. I realized that if I wanted to get an education in business, I should have skipped college, found a mentor, and started a business.

I think that college can be a valuable experience. For me, it was. But today the price must be weighed against the benefit. A diploma is only valued against the others that also have that same diploma. It is simple "supply and demand." If everyone has it, it is not worth anything. And today, I see people graduating from college with $50,000 - $100,000+ in student loans, and they can't get a job, making their diploma worthless.

Personally, if I had children, I would teach them to build wealth using OPM to invest—so they *never* need a diploma, and never need a job.

College funding is another topic for another book, and many books and articles have been written about "the best ways to fund your kid's college." I can hear the talking heads now, "Here is how to find the best 529 plan… blah blah blah."

But I think that teaching your kids how OPM works is far more important than giving advice on how to fund your kid's college.

Here is how I would summarize college today, as it relates to OPM:

- The students are told they need a diploma to get a good job.

- The teachers and the administrators need the students to borrow to pay for college.

- Without the student loans, the colleges would close, and the teachers and administrators would not have an income to pay off *their* student loans. Yes, they too were told they need to get a diploma to get a good job.

- The "banksters" are happy again to comply and lend money to these unsuspecting college students. But the banksters also know that many of the diplomas the students will receive will be worthless, so they must get a guarantee from the government (a guarantee from you, the taxpayer) that the students can never default on the loans.

- While in college and taking their student loans, they are told to *"save money and get good credit, and a student credit card is a great way to build credit."*

- The students save in the bank (providing OPM for the banksters to build their wealth.)

- The students also borrow on credit cards. This "OPM" to the students is temporary. And when interest rates kick in, the banks will again build their wealth.

- When the students graduate, they must try and find a job, as they have never been taught anything useful about building wealth. They need to make money quickly…to start paying back the banksters!

- And the process continues…

- The schools must continue teaching the students the "value of getting a college education to get a good job," so the teachers and administrators can have jobs, so they too can continue to pay back the banksters.

Do you see how this becomes a problem?

So, who's fault is it?

Is it the students who take the student loans?

Is it the teachers or administrators for encouraging them, and helping them fill out their applications?

Is it the banksters' fault for lending the money?

Is it the politicians' fault because the virtually unlimited amounts of money that can be lent to these unsuspecting college students—is guaranteed by the taxpayer?

Maybe it is the fault of corporations themselves that tell students, "To get a good job here, you must get a diploma"?

Okay, that's a lot of blame.

Rather than lay blame, let's see if we can all agree on this:

We live in a debt-matrix and the world runs on debt.

That debt can be used to make others wealthy, or it can be used to build wealth for yourself and your family.

It is up to you to decide how you want to use OPM.

Fortunately, today we are seeing some improvement regarding corporations requiring diplomas to get a job. Recently, Google, Ernst and Young, Costco, Hilton, Whole Foods, Apple, Starbucks, IBM, Tesla, Amazon, Publix, and many more corporations are not requiring a diploma to get a job. This is good news and a big step in the right direction.

Here is what I recommend to those that are uncertain if they should "go to school to get a safe and secure job."

If you want to work in a specific field, perhaps with one of the companies above, skip the diploma and do what you can to get your foot in the door. Work in the mail room, start at the reception desk, it doesn't matter, just get your foot in the door.

Companies today value experience far more than a diploma. Make friends in the industry and find a company that will actually promote you up through the ranks as you gain experience.

And, in your spare time, learn the basics of investing. Stay out of "bad debt" such as credit cards and auto loans. But learn to use "good debt", aka **OPM**, to make you money.

For me personally, the best "investment" I ever made was the time and money I put into getting my financial education.

You should learn of all the ways you too can build wealth using

OPM. And I hope that one day you will also be fortunate enough and will never rely on a job for your income.

16. Pay Off College Loans

My first advice is to try not to take them in the first place. But if you did, you will need to become a master at using OPM to invest. And use the investment profits, preferably tax-free profit, to pay them off.

You can read about how I paid off my student loans and credit card debt from college in "Rich Man Poor Bank." And, no, I didn't pay them off by "sending in extra payments." In fact, I did the opposite.

I sent in the minimums to my student loans and saved to buy real estate. I put 5% down on a piece of real estate and sold it two years later. I took the tax-free profit and cut a check to pay off all my debt, plus I netted a large tax-free profit which I used to buy more real estate.

What would have taken almost a decade or more of paying extra principal payments, I was able to accomplish in two years by using OPM.

You know what they say… "If you want better results, you should start asking better questions." I think a better question to ask should be: Is it better to go into debt to pay for college?

Or,

Is it better to take the four years you would spend in college, avoid the debt, and save up to buy some real estate, and harness the power of OPM to build wealth?

That is for each family to decide for themselves.

Business Planning

17. Key Person Insurance

The basics of key person insurance, or a "key man policy", is that a business or corporation can buy a life insurance policy on a key employee. If that employee were to pass away, a death benefit would be paid to the business or corporation that would be used to pay to find a replacement for that key employee.

Generally, term insurance is used for key person insurance. But, if you use an IUL all the other benefits described in this book can be available to the business owner, such as:

- Borrowing to pay off debt
- Borrowing to expand the business
- Borrowing in an economic downturn, without credit or income. And of course:
- Growing money without taxes
- Growing money without risk

Basically, you can **Build a Tax-Free Business Bank!** (see #21)

18. Employee Retention

IUL can be used as an employee retention plan.

Let's give you an example.

Let's say that you wanted to incentivize an employee to stay working with your company, perhaps until you sell it.

You could offer that employee a $250,000 bonus, paid to that employee only if they stay working with the company for ten years.

You could decide to fund an IUL with $45,000 a year for 5 years, totaling $225,000.

- This purchases approximately a $2,200,000 death benefit, paid to the company if that employee should die during the ten years.

- Because the IUL is owned by the company, the insurance, and the cash value would stay as an asset on the balance sheet until the employee is eligible for the bonus in year eleven.

- The cash value would grow tax-free, and risk-free inside the IUL.

- At year eleven, the business owner could take a tax-free loan of $250,000 and pay it to the employee. The bonus is taxable to the employee, but a tax-deduction to the business.

The company then keeps any remaining cash value still growing inside the IUL as a company asset. And if the employee passes away, even after leaving the company, the company receives the tax-free death benefit.

19. Buy/Sell Agreements

Let's define Buy/Sell Agreements:

A buy/sell agreement is a legally binding contract that defines how a partner's share of a business may be reassigned if that partner dies. Most often, the buy/sell agreement stipulates that the available shares be sold to the remaining partner/s, or to the partnership if one of the partners dies.

A life insurance policy is placed in force for each of the partners. In the event of death of a partner, the death benefit would be used to purchase those shares of the business at a predetermined price, so the remaining partner/s own the shares of the deceased partner—while also saving the deceased partner's family from the burden of finding a buyer, or negotiating a purchase price.

Either Term or IUL can be used to fund a buy/sell agreement.

20. Employers Can "Discriminate"

When a business is beginning to grow, it may not yet be profitable enough to offer a retirement plan to all the employees, which is mandatory with 401(k)s and other retirement plans.

Because an IUL is not a "retirement plan," it is not regulated as such and none of the same rules apply.

This is where an IUL becomes useful:

An owner may want to setup a plan for themselves, and perhaps offer to fund an IUL as an "executive bonus" for only certain employees.

The owner can setup an IUL and fund it at any amount for themselves. They then can pick and choose which employees they want to offer the executive bonus, and decide to fund each one, at any amount, without having to offer equal amounts to all of the employees.

21. Tax-Free Business Bank

We briefly touched on Tax-Free Business Bank in #17, "Key Person Insurance." But depending on the size of the business, it may also be beneficial to setup a corporate-owned life insurance plan, or "COLI" plan. COLI plans can be beneficial for retaining employees, growing the value of the business, and keeping liquidity while the business is growing.

Because COLI plans provide insurance for groups of employees, they can provide a lot more life insurance for less cost, as these plans are institutionally priced rather than retail priced.

Since the topic of COLI is quite large to cover, with different benefits depending if your business is setup as a "C" or "S" Corporation, you should consult with a CPA and insurance professional that understands both the tax, and other potential benefits of using an IUL to grow the value of your business.

Either using individual IULs owned by the business, or a Key Person IUL (also owned by the business), or a COLI plan, there are many ways to access cash via borrowing from the insurance company secured by the cash value of the plan, or by borrowing from a bank using the insurance cash value as collateral for the loan.

Many different types of insurance plans can be a valuable asset for any business when borrowing to expand the business.

PART THREE:
4 WAYS TO PROTECT IT!

Protecting Your Retirement Accounts

22. Supplemental Tax-Free Retirement Income

Let's look at an example of how an IUL can be used to provide **tax-free** retirement income to supplement your **taxable** retirement income.

It is important to remember that retirement accounts such as 401(k) and IRAs are funded pre-tax. This means that you get a tax-deduction on the contribution, the account grows tax-free, but you will be taxed at full ordinary income tax rates (yes, the highest form of taxes) on all your retirement income.

Yes, more taxes... year after year... for the rest of your life.

An IUL, similar to a Roth IRA is funded with after-tax income, grows with no taxes, and can provide supplemental tax-free income.

That's right, **no taxes**...year after year...for the rest of your life.

Let's take an example of Sarah Smart. She is 35 years old and wants to retire at age 67. She wants as much income as possible, and she understands the importance of reducing taxes on her retirement income.

Sarah earns $100,000 a year and decides to contribute 5%, or $5,000 toward retirement and receives the full match of 5% from her employer - another $5,000 (yes, that's OPM). $10,000 a year is socked-away toward her retirement.

At retirement, Sarah has accumulated $1,364,000 in her retirement plan. That is assuming that she earns 8% compounded *during all the 32 years she contributes to the plan.*

Assuming an income of 5% annually can be taken from the $1,364,000, this will generate about $68,200 of taxable income each year when she begins her retirement.

Now, let's estimate taxes will reduce that income by about 18%, reducing her income to $56,000 (depending on many, many factors – including if taxes rise, if she is paying state taxes, and if there are any deductions in her retirement – her income tax rate could be higher or lower.)

I have to ask: is $56,000 enough income to live the lifestyle you want in *your* retirement? I'm assuming the answer is, "No, not even close!"

Sarah also wanted more retirement income. So, she decided to start funding an IUL with $10,000 a year until age 66. She also wanted life insurance before and during her retirement, and understood the value of long-term care insurance for asset protection—including protecting the balance of her 401(k) during her retirement.

For 31 years, Sarah contributed $10,000 a year, which purchased her life insurance of $500,000 while also saving for the future. Her policy also provided LTC as a rider.

See chart on next page...

Accumulation phase

Age	Year	Premium	Before-tax policy income	After-tax policy income	Net surrender value	Death benefit
					Current charges	
36	1	$10,000	$0	$0	$0	$507,744
37	2	$10,000	$0	$0	$7,592	$516,147
38	3	$10,000	$0	$0	$16,500	$525,055
39	4	$10,000	$0	$0	$27,022	$534,507
40	5	$10,000	$0	$0	$38,134	$544,550
41	6	$10,000	$0	$0	$50,364	$555,711
42	7	$10,000	$0	$0	$63,404	$567,682
43	8	$10,000	$0	$0	$77,328	$580,536
44	9	$10,000	$0	$0	$92,200	$594,339
45	10	$10,000	$0	$0	$108,092	$609,161
46	11	$10,000	$0	$0	$126,181	$626,181
47	12	$10,000	$0	$0	$144,447	$644,447
48	13	$10,000	$0	$0	$164,032	$664,032
49	14	$10,000	$0	$0	$185,051	$685,051
50	15	$10,000	$0	$0	$207,616	$707,616
51	16	$10,000	$0	$0	$232,309	$732,309
52	17	$10,000	$0	$0	$258,835	$758,835
53	18	$10,000	$0	$0	$287,355	$787,355
54	19	$10,000	$0	$0	$318,018	$818,018
55	20	$10,000	$0	$0	$350,969	$850,969
56	21	$10,000	$0	$0	$386,380	$886,380
57	22	$10,000	$0	$0	$424,460	$924,460
58	23	$10,000	$0	$0	$465,416	$965,416
59	24	$10,000	$0	$0	$509,474	$1,009,474
60	25	$10,000	$0	$0	$556,989	$1,009,474
61	26	$10,000	$0	$0	$608,181	$1,009,474
62	27	$10,000	$0	$0	$663,338	$1,009,474
63	28	$10,000	$0	$0	$722,773	$1,009,474
64	29	$10,000	$0	$0	$786,831	$1,009,474
65	30	$10,000	$0	$0	$855,799	$1,044,075
66	31	$10,000	$0	$0	$930,089	$1,116,107
Total		$310,000				

At age 66, she made a total contribution of $310,000, and the death benefit rose to $1,116,107. Sarah had accumulated $930,086 in her IUL.

At age 67, she can start taking an annual income of **$75,000 tax-free** to supplement her taxable retirement income.

Income phase

Age	Year	Premium	Before-tax policy income	After-tax policy income	Current charges Net surrender value	Death benefit
67	32	$0	$75,000	$75,000	$925,395	$1,101,220
68	33	$0	$75,000	$75,000	$923,732	$1,090,003
69	34	$0	$75,000	$75,000	$921,926	$1,078,654
70	35	$0	$75,000	$75,000	$919,967	$1,067,161
71	36	$0	$75,000	$75,000	$917,825	$1,065,966
72	37	$0	$75,000	$75,000	$915,501	$1,053,767
73	38	$0	$75,000	$75,000	$912,989	$1,038,579
74	39	$0	$75,000	$75,000	$910,289	$1,020,278
75	40	$0	$75,000	$75,000	$907,411	$998,746
76	41	$0	$75,000	$75,000	$904,372	$973,867
77	42	$0	$75,000	$75,000	$901,013	$974,878
78	43	$0	$75,000	$75,000	$897,296	$975,650
79	44	$0	$75,000	$75,000	$893,169	$976,133
80	45	$0	$75,000	$75,000	$888,573	$976,267
81	46	$0	$75,000	$75,000	$883,431	$975,976
82	47	$0	$75,000	$75,000	$877,620	$975,136
83	48	$0	$75,000	$75,000	$871,104	$973,714
84	49	$0	$75,000	$75,000	$863,748	$971,573
85	50	$0	$75,000	$75,000	$855,387	$968,544
86	51	$0	$75,000	$75,000	$845,804	$964,404
87	52	$0	$75,000	$75,000	$834,824	$958,975
88	53	$0	$75,000	$75,000	$822,198	$952,000
89	54	$0	$75,000	$75,000	$807,544	$943,085
90	55	$0	$75,000	$75,000	$790,683	$932,047
91	56	$0	$75,000	$75,000	$771,041	$918,288
92	57	$0	$75,000	$75,000	$750,315	$872,941
93	58	$0	$75,000	$75,000	$728,684	$824,374
94	59	$0	$75,000	$75,000	$706,911	$773,270
95	60	$0	$75,000	$75,000	$685,636	$720,149
96	61	$0	$75,000	$75,000	$665,988	$665,988
97	62	$0	$75,000	$75,000	$644,800	$644,800
98	63	$0	$75,000	$75,000	$621,985	$621,985
99	64	$0	$75,000	$75,000	$597,418	$597,418
100	65	$0	$75,000	$75,000	$570,966	$570,966
Total			$2,550,000	$2,550,000		

So, if Sarah were to live to be age 100, she would receive a total of **$2,550,000** of tax-free income from her IUL.

Let's not forget that she is also still receiving income from her retirement account, on top of this.

So, when we add up her **total** annual income—the $56,000 of after-tax income from her retirement plan, and the $75,000 tax-free income from her IUL—she would receive a total of $131,000 income each year, after tax!

And, Sarah would still leave a tax-free death benefit of **$570,966** to her heirs.

That adds up to over $3 million, 100% tax-free! Pretty cool, right?

And, as we mentioned, if Sarah ever gets sick and needs long-term care, her IUL LTC rider can help protect her 401(k) and other assets, by not forcing her to liquidate them to pay for long-term care costs.

Now…I don't think Sarah will get social security, but this seems like the perfect time to add the potential taxes on your social security benefits.

Jump to #23 if you trust that the social security "trust fund" will be around to provide another source of supplemental retirement income.

23. Tax-Free Social Security

I'm making the assumption that the social security trust fund will still pay a benefit to most Americans during their retirement. Personally, I don't expect a penny from social security.

If you are below 50, I would also encourage you to do your planning assuming you will not get any money from the social security trust fund, as it is drastically underfunded by 2034.

As they say, "It is better to have it and not need it, than to need it and not have it."

If you are reading this and you are between the ages of 50 and

65, this may be an important topic for you. It may provide more income in retirement by reducing the taxes you have to pay during your retirement and help you protect the assets you have.

Did you know that when the government started social security in 1935, they **promised** that you would receive your social security tax-free?

And do you remember when they decided to change the rules and make it taxable to most Americans?

Well, that happened in 1984.

But as you read about in *Top 10 Ways to Avoid Taxes,* social security benefits are not taxable to everyone… they are only taxable to those that don't know how to avoid the taxes—regardless of the amount of income that they receive. This is understanding what is defined as "Provisional Income."

Provisional income is defined as the types of income you receive that will trigger taxation of your social security benefits. Income from a job and/or income from retirement accounts can trigger taxes on your social security benefits.

Here is what is important to know:

Income from Roth IRAs and income from IULs are **both tax-exempt**, and both don't trigger taxation of your social security benefits. So, you can take as much income from your IUL and Roth IRA and still collect all your social security income tax-free.

This could be three sources of 100% tax-free retirement income!

Since this is a big topic alone, I'm going to recommend a book called "The Power of Zero: How to Get to the 0% Tax Bracket and Transform Your Retirement."

In this amazing book, author and CPA David McKnight describes the strategies for retiring and paying 0% taxes on all your retirement income. He describes how it may be beneficial to move a portion of your taxable retirement accounts to non-taxable retirement accounts, such as Roth IRA and IUL.

As McKnight points out, taxes are historically low when compared to tax rates in the past. And tax rates must rise to fund the trillions of unfunded liabilities promised to Americans, such as social security, Medicare and Medicaid.

As of today, here is what David McKnight and I both believe: **"Taxes will rise once again in 5 years, 8 months, and 18 days."** (At the end of 2025)

How about you?

Where do you think taxes are going?

1. Do you believe that taxes will go up in 2025?

Did you answer Yes? Or no?

2. Do you believe that the government will raise taxes again before your retirement? Yes? Or no?

3. Do you believe that the government could continue to raise taxes during the 25 to 30+ years of your retirement? Yes? Or no?

If you answered yes to the above, the strategy described in David McKnight's book may be beneficial to you, and even more so if combined with the CARES Act. What makes this topic so much more intriguing is that coronavirus opened the door for many Americans to potentially pay less in taxes during their retirement.

Here is how:

The current CARES (Coronavirus Aid, Relief, and Economic Security) Act allows penalty-free distributions from your taxable retirement accounts. It doesn't waive the taxes, but it does allow you to spread the tax burden over 3 years.

So now that you have learned about the benefits of IUL—and you feel like taxes may rise in the future – this could be an opportunity to remove a portion from your taxable retirement accounts, pay the taxes over three years, and build more tax-free retirement income… while at the same time securing life insurance and LTC for asset protection.

REMEMBER:

The same rules that apply to banks also apply to taxes.

Financial Education ▼ = Taxes ▲

Financial Education ▲ = Taxes ▼

When I learned these rules—and that the government can change them anytime they want—I made a rule for myself:

I'll never fund a single penny into a traditional retirement account "to save money on taxes."

I only invest in accounts that grow highly tax-advantaged, or 100% tax-free.

They can earn high rates of returns, and I must be able to use OPM in my investing to generate even higher returns.

I can access tax-free distributions regardless of my age, and I can re-invest again in other tax-exempt investments.

The good news is, you can do it too!

24. Never Invest Conservatively Again!

Let me introduce you to two different investors, who took very different paths in their retirement planning:

Albert had accumulated $1,000,000 in his retirement account.

Over a 24-month period, Albert experienced a 50% stock market crash, leaving him with only **$500,000** in his retirement account. **A 50% loss**!

Barbara had only accumulated $500,000 in her retirement account,

But also had $400,000 in an IUL, totaling **$900,000**.

Barbara experienced the same 50% stock market crash, leaving her with $250,000 in her retirement account.

But her IUL did not crash and remained at $400,000, totaling $650,000. **A 28% loss.**

So, which investor would you rather be?

Albert, losing 50% of all his retirement savings. **OR**
Barbara, losing 28% of all her retirement savings.

Now, before you answer, here is some additional information:

When the market finally recovers, Albert will recover back to the $1,000,000 in his retirement account.

Barbara will also recover back to **$500,000** in her retirement account.

But let me give you more good news about Barbara.

Even if Barbara's IUL only experiences 50% of the recovery, due to caps on many IULs, Barbara will now have $600,000 in her IUL, totaling **$1,100,000**.

If Barbara had a Next Generation IUL, she could actually outperform the market in the recovery, and grow her IUL to $800,000+, and have a total portfolio of **$1,300,000+**.

There is even more to this story…

History tells us two things about investor behavior:

1. Albert is far more likely to sell during the crash when experiencing a 50% decline in his overall portfolio…and may never recover back to the $1,000,000. And,

2. Albert is also far more likely to blend his portfolio with bonds, both before and during his retirement to reduce the chance of "losing 50%" (again).

This is just another example how an IUL can be used to reduce fear, and by understanding the power of not losing money, you can earn even higher returns on your overall portfolio.

Should we also mention taxes?

Albert would have $1,000,000 taxable.

Barbara would have $500,000 taxable. But Barbara's $600,000 to $800,000+ would be tax-free!

Let's jump into another example of how an IUL can help you manage risk, reduce fear, and help you turn $1,000,000 in retirement savings to almost $3,600,000 million at age 85, rather than $444,000.

25. Maximize Retirement by Minimizing Losses

Let's evaluate the current advice from the financial industry and the talking heads.

The industry "experts" say, "You should invest 100% in stocks to get the full long-term returns of the market."

They also say, "You should invest 100% in stocks when you are younger, then move more of your money into bonds as you get closer to retirement to reduce the risk."

But if you take this advice, you must ignore their previous advice… and you will ensure you don't get the full long-term returns of the market.

Finally, when you retire, the "experts" say, "In retirement, you should keep your portfolio 60% in stocks and 40% in bonds (60/40) to reduce the risk of losses—as losses, when taking distributions, can cause you to run out of money in retirement."

They then add, "If you stay 100% in stocks, you will also get higher overall returns in retirement, and have less chance of running out of money."

Finally, they say, "Because you are only 60/40 and won't get the full returns of the market, you can only take 4% out per year out of your retirement, or risk running out of money."

First of all, why does it seem the experts—many times the same people—give advice one day, and then the opposite advice the next?

My guess is so that they can say they were right some of the time.

This whole "running out of money" presents a dilemma.

To solve this dilemma, let me introduce you to a term called "Sequence of Returns."

Sequence of Returns notes that "market losses, particularly in early retirement, can erode the overall portfolio—specifically when taking money out of the portfolio after a market decline."

Basically, if you take out money from your retirement account after a crash, sequence of returns says you are far more likely to run out of money in your retirement.

So, here's the rule:

Don't take money out of your retirement account on the years the market is negative.

To give an example of sequence of returns, let's introduce you to Tom.

Tom knew that keeping his money 100% in stocks **prior** to retirement would grow his retirement account much larger, but also that keeping his retirement 100% in stocks **during** his retirement would also help him not run out of money.

Fortunately for Tom, he discovered how an IUL could help him not run out of money, and at the same time help him grow his retirement account, both prior to and during retirement.

Tom's plan was to fund an IUL at the same time as funding his 401(k). At age 65, Tom had $1,000,000 in his retirement. The cash value in his IUL had grown to $233,000.

Tom's strategy was simple:

A. Any years the market is negative, he would not remove money from his retirement account.

B. For income in the down years, he would access tax-free distributions from his IUL until his retirement account has recovered.

C. Only after the market has recovered, would he then continue to take money out of his retirement account, allowing his IUL to grow again.

After 20 years, Tom's plan would pay off!

Let's see the comparison of Tom's plan with an IUL to hedge against sequence of returns, rather than if he had not used it.

Without an IUL

At 65, Tom starts taking $70,000 each year from his retirement account (7% distribution). But immediately the market then crashes for two years. With Tom taking distributions each year, his account shrinks to **$531,594 by age 66**.

The sequence of returns makes a difference. Losses early in retirement can particularly hurt Tom's overall retirement pool.

Retirement Account

Age	Beginning of Year Balance	Annual Withdrawal	Post Withdrawal Balance	Hypothetical S&P 500® Return	End of Year Balance
65	**$1,000,000**	$70,000	$930,000	-14.66%	$793,662
66	$793,662	-$70,700	$722,962	-26.47%	**$531,594**
67	$531,594	-$71,407	$460,187	37.20%	$631,377
68	$631,377	-$72,121	$559,255	23.84%	$692,090
69	$692,582	-$72,842	$619,740	-7.16%	**$575,366**
70	$575,366	-$73,571	$501,796	6.56%	$534,713
71	$534,713	-$74,306	$501,796	18.44%	$545,306
72	$545,306	-$75,049	$470,257	32.50%	$623,090
73	$623,090	-$75,800	$547,290	-4.92%	**$520,363**
74	$520,363	-$76,558	$443,805	21.55%	$539,445
75	$539,445	-$77,324	$462,122	22.56%	$566,376
76	$566,376	-$78,097	$488,280	6.27%	$518,895
77	$518,895	-$78,878	$440,017	31.73%	$579, 35
78	$579,635	-$79,667	$499,968	18.67%	$593,312
79	$593,312	-$80,463	$512,849	5.25%	$539,773
80	$539,773	-$81,268	$458,506	16.61%	$534,663
81	$534,663	-$82,081	$452,583	31.96%	$596,006
82	$596,006	-$82,901	$513,105	-3.11%	**$497,147**
83	$497,147	-$83,730	$413,417	30.47%	$539,385
84	$539,385	-$84,568	$454,818	7.62%	$489,475
85	$489,475	-$85,413	$404,01	10.08%	**$444,791**

The S&P® period reflected here runs from 1973-1993 to show the effect of starting in a negative timeframe followed by positive return. This also shows the impact of starting retirement at a later point in time 1990-2010 to show the effect of retirement in a positive period of market returns followed by an extended period of market losses.

In 20 years Tom's portfolio is reduced by nearly 56%. He can reduce his withdrawals but it will affect his retirement goals.

Past performance of the S&P 500® Index is no guarantee of future results. Clients cannot invest directly into the S&P 500® Index. The Wall Street Journal echoes these concerns. It's what they call the Sequence of Returns —noting that market losses, particularly early in retirement, can erode the overall portfolio and affect long term retirement funds.[5]

If Tom continues taking those 7% annual distributions, he locks in the losses in the down years, and has only $444,791 remaining in his retirement account at age 85.

The experts were right, Tom is at risk of running out of money!

With an IUL

Rather than remove the money from his retirement account in the down years, Tom took a tax-free distribution from his IUL. But because the funds from his IUL are tax-free, he doesn't need to take out the full $70,000, rather he only needs to take $50,000 to net the same amount.

The market declined for two years, and Tom took no money out of his retirement account. He resumed distributions from his retirement at 68, after the market recovered.

At age 70, the market again experienced a negative year, and again Tom accessed his IUL rather than touching his retirement—allowing his retirement account to recover. Again, in other down years – at age 74 and 83 – Tom used his IUL for income rather than his retirement account.

By simply turning off withdrawals from his retirement funds in only 5 of 20 years, Tom can have a dramatic change in his retirement assets.

Tom's policy cash surrender values offer a source of funds for those 5 years. He takes withdrawals from his life insurance policy only in years that follow market losses. This avoids selling into losses.

| | Retirement Account | | | | | Life Insurance Policy | | | |
Age	Beginning of Year Balance	Annual Withdrawal	Post Withdrawal Balance	Hypothetical S&P 500® Return	End of Year Balance	Annual Premiums	Death Benefit	Tax-Free Withdrawal /loans	End of Year Cash Value
65	$1,000,000	($70,000)	$930,000	-14.66%	$793,662	$6967	$500,000	$0	$233,000
66	$793,662		$793,662	-26.47%	$583,580	$0	$450,000	($50,000)	$195,000
67	$583,580		$583,580	37.20%	$800,671	$0	$400,000	($50,000)	$155,100
68	$800,671	($72,121)	$728,550	23.84%	$902,237	$0	$400,000		$165,000
69	$902,237	($72,842)	$829,394	-7.16%	$770,010	$0	$400,000		$176,000
70	$770,010		$770,010	6.56%	$820,522	$0	$350,000	($50,000)	$133,000
71	$820,522	($74,306)	$746,216	18.44%	$883,818	$0	$350,500		$141,000
72	$883,818	($75,049)	$808,769	32.50%	$1,071,618	$0	$349,000		$148,000
73	$1,071,618	($75,800)	$995,819	-4.92%	$946,824	$0	$349,000		$156,000
74	$946,824		$946,824	21.55%	$1,150,865	$0	$293,000	($55,000)	$106,000
75	$1,150,865	($77,324)	$1,073,541	22.56%	$1,315,732	$0	$291,000		$110,000
76	$1,315,732	($78,097)	$1,237,635	6.27%	$1,315,235	$0	$290,000		$114,000
77	$1,315,235	($78,878)	$1,236,357	31.73%	$1,628,654	$0	$288,500		$119,000
78	$1,628,654	($79,667)	$1,548,987	18.67%	$1,838,183	$0	$287,000		$123,000
79	$1,838,183	($80,463)	$1,757,720	5.25%	$1,850,000	$0	$286,000		$127,000
80	$1,850,000	($81,268)	$1,768,732	16.61%	$2,062,519	$0	$284,000		$132,000
81	$2,062,519	($82,081)	$1,980,438	31.69%	$2,608,039	$0	$283,000		$137,000
82	$2,608,039	($82,901)	$2,525,138	-3.11%	$2,446,606	$0	$281,000		$143,000
83	$2,446,606		$2,446,606	30.47%	$3,192,087	$0	$218,000	($60,000)	$84,000
84	$3,192,087	($84,568)	$3,107,519	7.62%	$3,344,312	$0	$215,000		$85,000
85	$3,344,312	($85,413)	$3,258,899	10.08%	$3,587,396	$0	$213,000		$86,000

By turning off access in 5 critical years, and not selling into losses, Tom's assets have now shifted from $444,791 to an amount just over $3,587,000 - adding a cushion to Tom's retirement.

Tom is still able to leave a legacy for his family.

Tom, at age 85 slept well with $3,587,396 in his retirement.

Tom could enjoy his retirement, never worry about running out of money, and pass more money to his heirs.

What a difference!

This is just another example of how an IUL can provide protection both before you die, but also protection from running out of money during retirement, and help you pass millions more to your heirs, simply by understanding sequence of returns.

What about before retirement?

This same example can be used before retirement to pass on millions more! The strategy is similar, but with one exception:

Grow your money in an IUL, and when the markets crash, borrow from your IUL and fund more money into stocks and ETFs to purchase more shares when they are cheap.

If you think that this strategy is powerful just for not taking distributions from your retirement account, it is far more powerful when adding more money to a stock portfolio, especially when using OPM!

You can earn the returns in **both** the IUL and the stock portfolio when the market recovers!

PART FOUR:
YOUR LEGACY!

Legacy Planning
(Bonus Way #26!)

26. Pass a Large Death Benefit to Your Family, Tax-Free and Probate-Free

The most obvious benefit of life insurance is a death benefit when you die.

What is lesser known is that the life insurance, plus the investments – yes, including all the growth – is passed to your heirs tax-free. And the death benefit plus the growth avoids probate. This means that the government can't lock-up your assets in the probate courts and start applying their fees, taxes, etc.

As I wrote about in Top 10 Ways to Avoid Taxes, "Chapter 11 - "Die," life insurance, real estate and stocks can be passed to heirs, 100% tax-free. However, very few investments avoid probate.

Let's look at Taxation and Probate with those assets, compared to life insurance.

REAL ESTATE

No Taxes :) Real Estate receives a "step up in basis" and can be passed to heirs tax-free. Good News!

But Probate : (If there are debts that are owed at time of death, such as large medical debts or past taxes, while in probate, the real estate can be liquidated to pay those debts.

STOCK ACCOUNTS

No Taxes :) Stock accounts receive a "step up in basis" and can be passed to heirs tax-free.

But Probate : (Again, if there are debts that must be paid, such as large medical bills or past taxes, the stock accounts can be liquidated to pay those debts.

LIFE INSURANCE

No Taxes :) As we said before, life insurance, and the investments inside them can be passed to heirs tax-free.

And, No Probate :) If there are debts that are owed upon death, such as large medical bills or past taxes, the life insurance death benefit, and the cash value can be passed to the heirs tax-free. The government…and the medical bill collectors are, as they say, "SOL" (Sorry, Out of Luck).

The life insurance checks will arrive to your beneficiaries, without taxes, without probate, and hassle-free![1]

---

1 Note: State and Federal laws change, and the laws may have changed when you read this book. The laws can also be different from state to state. Be sure to consult with a licensed estate planning attorney to review your situation.

DON'T FORGET THE RING!

The most important part to remember when considering an IUL, or any permanent insurance policy is this:

Treat it like you are GETTING MARRIED!

You will be stuck with your decision for many years (10 to 15 years depending on your surrender period) and in some cases, "till death do us part."

So do your research and be sure to get educated about the costs, benefits, and flexibility of the IUL.

The wrong spouse can cost you a fortune, in both gains and costs, not to mention your sanity. The wrong insurance policy can increase your costs and reduce your potential gains, which overall will cause more taxes!

Yes, you can (eventually) get divorced, but it will be expensive, and can cost you a fortune, and perhaps many, many years of lost time, which you can never get back. "Till death do us part" they say…hopefully it does not kill you!

I'm sure you would agree that it is important to find the right spouse. It is also important to find the right IUL…for an incredibly rewarding and lifelong "marriage."

You should probably ask lots of questions to your potential spouse before tying the knot, so here are the questions you should ask about your potential IUL, before getting "married."

The Top 10
Questions to Ask

Before Getting Hitched to Your IUL!

1. What is the purpose of this IUL for me?

Of course the first and main purposes of an IUL are both permanent life insurance and long-term care for asset protection. But what are your other purposes in purchasing an IUL?

Do we want to use an alternative no-loss investment strategy to complement our stocks, bonds, and real estate?

Will it be used to provide a down payment to buy real estate?

Is it to provide a down payment to our son/daughter when they want to buy a home?

Do we want to use this for college funding or education costs?

Is it to provide a tax-free supplemental retirement income?

Will we use it to start a business?

Do we want to borrow to invest in the stock market or purchase other investments when the prices are low?

Is it to shelter a tax-free inheritance back into tax-exempt investments?

Do we want to build it to pay off our real estate before retirement?

Will it be used as an executive bonus plan for my business?

Will it provide an incentive to keep our best employees?

Or maybe your purpose is something completely different?

2. Is the insurance agent "captive?"

If the agent's company name on their business card is the same as on the policy they are selling, they may be captive. You should ask, and be sure to compare policies from a competitor. If an agent can only sell for that company, that is a conflict of interest. But even if they are not captive, this should be your next question:

3. Is the insurance company publicly traded?

If you are shopping for groceries, it doesn't matter if the store you are shopping at is publicly traded. The price you pay is the price you pay, and it is easy to compare.

But in general, if a corporation is publicly traded, they have a responsibility to create profitability to their shareholders, and many times that profit comes in the form of more charges to their customers. That's simply another conflict of interest when buying a financial product, but most important when you may own it for the rest of your life.

The reason that I use both a credit union and a bank, is I make them compete for my business. Credit unions are owned by the members, but I also use a big bank for my airmiles/rewards as they give me more "free stuff" than my credit union.

In my research, I've found that many of the insurance companies that are publicly traded don't have the best policies, either for term or IUL. Even in the case of term insurance, if a company is the "cheapest," it may be because the policy is not convertible (less claims paid = more profits for the shareholders).

And, who builds the risk-free portfolios? Are they publicly traded?

Let's take it a step further with IUL. Some of the smaller insurance companies say they are a "mutual benefit insurance company", but they are too small to build the risk-free portfolios themselves, so they must hire a megabank to build the portfolio for them. And yes, that megabank must also maximize profit to their shareholders. This could result in lower caps, and/or higher fees in an IUL.

4. What are the riders and their costs?

There are many riders that can be added to an IUL. Think of a rider as an add-on to your car, like an upgrade to the stereo system, or even adding additional horsepower.

LTC riders are becoming more common, but many smaller insurance companies don't have this option. In my opinion, you are not getting the maximum value of an IUL without this inexpensive form of asset protection.

Some riders like terminal illness/chronic illness are free within IULs (many advance a portion of the death benefit if you only have 12 months to live).

As we cover in detail below, riders now exist to supercharge the growth in your IUL cash value for even greater returns.

5. Is the Long-Term Care "indemnity"?

In the past, traditional LTC would require not only being very sick but also that the caregiver send receipts in the mail to the insurance company and request reimbursements for medical expenses. They were called "reimbursement" policies as they only covered the cost of care.

Fortunately, today, the LTC riders on most IULs are "indemnity" plans which don't require sending receipts in the mail. They simply pay a monthly benefit based on the amount of insurance.

For example, if a person owns an IUL with a $500,000 death benefit and qualifies for LTC, they can collect 2% of the death benefit each month – in this case, up to $10,000 a month. The money can be spent however they want, it can even go to a savings account for additional reserves.

If the insured uses the LTC rider for 6 months, then recovers and no longer needs the help, they would simply turn off the benefit. They would have used $60,000 of the death benefit, and the remaining amount of $440,000 will remain to pay as either a death benefit, or for future LTC coverage.

IUL LTC benefits typically pay out based on the ability to perform "ADLs" or Activities of Daily Living. These are things like bathing, taking medication, mobility, feeding, etc. Needing help for "two of the five ADLs" will generally qualify you for the LTC benefit.

6. How high are the caps? Any uncapped strategies?

Most IULs have caps, but only a handful of insurance companies have developed uncapped strategies. The downside with an uncapped strategy is that you won't get the first 5% of the rise in the market, but it will also remove the cap on growth. So, if the market rises by 30%, you could net 25%!

I've found the most competitive (mutual) insurance companies have the highest caps, and uncapped strategies.

You may also want to ask, "How often has the insurance company reduced caps in the past?"

The most competitive insurance companies that also build their own portfolios are less likely to reduce caps.

7. Does this IUL have alternate loan options?

IULs traditionally have had only fixed rate or traditional loan options.

Fixed Rate or Traditional Loan Option

A fixed rate loan is where you can borrow from your IUL and pay 2-3% interest. At the same time, the insurance company takes the amount borrowed out of your cash value and places it in an interest-bearing account where it also earns you 2-3% interest.

In effect, you're paying very little or no interest for "borrowing" that money. But, in doing so, those funds you borrowed **don't participate in any of the upside growth of the market.**

It is easy to think of this like a "withdrawal" (although you are taking a loan).

Let's say that you had $100,000 in your IUL and wanted to take a fixed rate loan of $50,000. You would receive the $50,000 – no taxes – but your policy cash value is reduced to $50,000. The participation you have for any growth in your IUL that year is only on that remaining $50,000.

If your IUL earned 15% that year, it would only be credited $7,500.

Variable or Alternate Loan Option

The other option is a variable rate loan, or "participating" or "alternate" loan option. This means you will pay an interest rate on the loan (perhaps 4-5%), but your full cash value would remain in the markets for any potential growth..

In this case, if you had $100,000 in your IUL, and borrowed the $50,000 using the alternate loan, you would receive the $50,000—again, tax-free—and still have the full $100,000 in your IUL participating in any upside that year.

- When borrowing the $50,000 at 5% interest, at the end of the year you would owe the insurance company $2,500.

- But if your IUL earned 15%, the insurance company would credit $15,000 in your cash value! That $50,000 which remained in your policy, earned you an extra $7,500 that year!

Would you like to pay $2,500 to earn $7,500?

This is the power of OPM. And more good news is that the interest you owe can be paid straight from the gains in your policy cash value.

If you want to "Build Your Own Tax-Free Family Bank," you must have both fixed and variable ("alternate") loan options available in your IUL.

Then you can decide when taking the loans:

"Do I want it fixed rate option and **not** participate in the market?"

or,

"Do I want to borrow at the 5% rate, and keep all my money growing in the potential upside of the market?"

8. Cost vs. Benefit. Can I supercharge it?

Think of a rider like upgrading your stereo system, or in the case of an IUL, "supercharging" the IUL by adding horsepower.

For Tesla lovers, it's the "ludicrous" mode.

I've only found one insurance company where you can pay a fee to supercharge your IUL to have far greater upside… potentially twice that of the market return!

If you don't want the extra fee for that additional performance the next year, you can turn off the rider. Using this feature wisely, and weighing risk vs reward, it can translate into far greater tax-free profit!

Always ask, when looking for an IUL:

- Are no-cap strategies available?
- Can I supercharge my IUL for greater growth potential of the market?

9. Surrender Schedule (Is there a Prenup?)

If you are getting married to an IUL, you will also want to know how long you are "stuck" with the IUL. Simply ask, "How long is the surrender period before I can move my money to a new IUL?" The good news is that money can be moved tax-free from one permanent life insurance policy to another—even between different types of permanent insurance policies. This is called a 1035 exchange.

So, if you bought an old Whole Life, Universal Life, or Variable Universal Life more than 10 years ago, you may want to look at the options for moving your money to a newer policy that has much greater benefits.

10. What are my options for premium financing?

Premium financing is when loans are taken from banks to fund IULs. This is another form of OPM and can be very effective for buying larger IULs. But this requires highly specialized expertise to know how to properly design and set one up.

All the factors above will come into play, as well as: "What are the costs to borrowing the money?" And "When is the IUL likely to pay back the loan, so I don't have to?"

Again, premium financing is only for "**HENRYs**" (High Earner, Not Rich Yet), "**HNW**" (High-Net-Worth individuals), and "**UHNW**" (Ultra-High-Net-Worth individuals).

Your IUL can bring you great security, and tax-free prosperity all at the same time! Now, if you have decided that an IUL might be right for you, would you like to practice your vows?...

YOUR VOWS

**I, (your name here), take you,
to be my IUL, to have and to hold, and to keep
you in a safe place, from this day forward,**

**For better or worse, in good markets,
and in bad, you will make us money, but not
lose any, regardless of how bad it gets,**

**And in tight times, if our income falls short,
you will help keep us safe, with tax-free
distributions prior to age 59½,**

**And in richer times, when our income rises,
you will grow our net worth, exempt from all
state, federal, and capital gains taxes,**

**In sickness you will protect us with long-
term care to protect our assets, and in death
you protect our investments from taxes,**

**But until death do us part...
You will grant us tax-free loans to invest
using "Other People's Money" (OPM), which
we will cherish and use wisely to invest again,
in real estate, and other appreciating assets,
to help us grow, protect and pass on
our wealth to our families that
we love very much, and to
the charities that we
support.**

PART FIVE:
CONCLUSION

In Summary

1. I value permanent life insurance, so when I die, my family gets a large tax-free benefit.

2. I also own convertible term insurance to keep costs down, which later can be converted to IULs to shelter more after-tax money.

3. I value the long-term care, so that if I got really sick (again) I would not be a financial burden to my family.

4. My income is rising, and I also believe that taxes will rise too, so my tax bill will grow larger each year on both my earned income, and investment profits. I guess you can say I'm a **HENRY**, a *High Earner, Not Rich Yet.*

5. I think of IULs like owning a **Tax-Free Family Bank**, where I can use OPM for my investing.

Here are the basics:

- I like to borrow money when the markets are bad, or have crashed, to either buy real estate, or stocks, or both.

- I can borrow at low rates. This is OPM first from the insurance company.

- If I were to buy real estate, then I'd be using OPM from the bank—which is OPM once again. For example, If I were to borrow the 20% down to buy real estate from my IUL, then borrow the other 80% from a bank, none of my own money would be in the investment!

- In IULs, the loans are secured by my cash value, so I don't have to get approved by a bank.

- This way, I'll still get the full returns on my IUL, plus the returns on the real estate or other investment.

I love OPM in my investing!

Never forget, OPM is the secret to building great wealth!

Well, I can't just end off here… I've simply got to tell you the other ways you can use OPM in your investing!

Bonus Report

The Best Ways You Can Use OPM in Your Investing!

Let's cover the other types of investments where investors can use OPM to help them build wealth.

401(k)

The first and easiest way to use OPM is when receiving a matching contribution on your 401(k).

Be sure to always get the full match available from your employer. That is adding the power of OPM, and a guaranteed 100% return on your money. You are using OPM—in this case your employer's money —which is "free money" for your investing.

Anything above what is matched, you don't get OPM. You need to decide if that is your best investment based on your goals.

Buy a Home

The second and most common way to use OPM is when buying a home.

You may put 10% as a down payment to buy a home, and your bank will lend you the other 90%. That is 10% your money, and 90% the bank's money. This is 90% OPM.

If you own a home, and get a match on your 401(k), you are already using OPM twice! Good job! It seems simple, doesn't it?

Here are a couple of other ways to use OPM:

Brokerage Accounts

You could open a brokerage account, buy stocks, mutual funds and ETFs, and request a "margin account," where you could borrow money to buy more stock. For example, you could purchase $10,000 of XYZ company, and then borrow $10,000 from the brokerage (called "margin") which can be used to buy an additional $10,000 of stock. You would have invested $10,000, and bought $20,000 of stock, potentially doubling your rate of return.

The **good news** is that when stocks rise, you could get double the rate of return.

The **bad news** is that if the market/stock prices begin to decline or crash, your broker may sell your stock to make sure you have enough money in your account to pay back the loan. This is referred to as a "margin call." Since your stock price would be decreasing, your broker has the right to start selling your position, at lower and lower prices to keep enough cash to pay back the margin loan. If done at the wrong time, you would buy high, and be forced to sell low, and sell even more if your portfolio continues to decline in value.

This is considered a dangerous way to invest—investing your money plus the broker's money. You can lose money twice as fast... and lock in the losses!

When taking a margin loan, your broker will charge you interest, similar to borrowing from an insurance company. **But if borrowing from your IUL, it is secured by your cash value which can't lose money, so it also can't trigger a margin call.**

Borrowing on margin is generally used by sophisticated investors, or investors under the guidance of an experienced advisor/trader.

Borrowing from an IUL is less risky, and the money doesn't have to be invested in the market. It can be invested in real estate, businesses, etc., to diversify your risk and portfolio.

Securities-Backed Line of Credit ("S-BLOC")

When funding an account with municipal bonds, mutual funds, ETFs, etc., it is possible for a specialized bank to open a line of credit (backed by your securities) where you can borrow money to be used for whatever purpose you want.

This could be invaluable if you own investments that have appreciated in value, and rather than selling them and have a tax liability, you can just take a loan. These credit lines are generally restricted to lower risk, more diversified investments such as mutual funds, ETFs, and bonds/muni bonds.

Evaluating, "can I use OPM?" helps me decide where I want to put my money. And…

- Most IRAs don't use OPM.
- Most Roth IRAs don't use OPM.
- SEP IRAs (for self-employed) don't use OPM.
- Contributing to a 401(k) that does not offer a match does not use OPM.
- Mutual fund investments typically don't use OPM.
- Real estate can use OPM.
- IUL can use OPM in many ways!

How many of your investments
are you using OPM?

Well, that's the end of this book. Did this give you some food for thought? Are you now on the hunt to find your perfect IUL "soulmate" to "marry" for the rest of your life?

I hope you find your perfect IUL partner, and that relationship grows stronger each year...and that you have a lifetime of love and happiness together!

I love my IUL!

**If you have additional questions
that I didn't answer here, or would like some
additional IUL advice or suggestions, feel free to**

email us at
10ways@remiigroup.com

Made in the USA
Coppell, TX
07 February 2021